Acquiring Editor: Jon Kolko
Development Editor: Jon Kolko
Project Manager: Jon Kolko/Paul Burke
Designer: Paul Burke
Illustrator: Austin Rucker

Brown Bear Publishing
1408 Cotton Street
Austin TX 78702

Notices
Knowledge and best practice in this field are constantly changing. As new research and experience broaden our understanding, changes in research methods or professional practices, may become necessary. Practitioners and researchers must always rely on their own experience and knowledge in evaluating and using any information or methods described herein. In using such information or methods they should be mindful of their own safety and the safety of others, including parties for whom they have a professional responsibility.

Library of Congress Cataloging-in-Publication Data

Kolko, Jon.

Creative Clarity : A practical guide for bringing creative thinking into your company / written by Jon Kolko

p. cm.

ISBN 978-0-9788538-1-5

1. Business 2. Product design. 3. Human-machine systems. 4. Human-computer interaction. 5. Engineering design.

Printed in the United States

11 12 13 14 15   10 9 8 7 6 5 4 3 2 1

For information on all Jon Kolko publications visit our website at www.jonkolko.com

CREATIVE CLARITY

JON KOLKO

CONTENTS

OVERVIEW

This book is built on a simple premise: **Most companies don't know what creativity really is, so they can't benefit from it.**

We look around at the few companies that seem to have creativity figured out, the companies celebrated as creative market leaders. Google has launched an entire business called "X" to drive its creative "moon shots"— huge problems with radical solutions. X is combining creatively diverse backgrounds in a high-pressure environment to arrive at massively different ways of thinking about problems: "What if a sculptor and a kite surfer worked together to rethink how we harness the power of the wind? Or if an aerospace engineer and a fashion designer teamed up to bring internet to everyone with balloons?" (X, 2016)

Disney, which is literally in the business of selling creativity, spent more than a billion dollars developing the MyMagic+ wristband and its supporting infrastructure. The ethos of creativity is fundamental to everything the company does, including shepherding in a digital era for its brand.

And Tesla, perhaps one of the most creative companies of our generation, is redefining multiple industries by pursuing a dramatic vision of the future. The company is so confident of that vision that CEO Elon Musk presents it on tesla.com: The "Master Plan" includes a focus on solar power, affordable vehicles, and autonomous driving. (Musk, 2016)

We see these companies' articulated solutions, glossy product launches, market-driving innovations, and blog post after blog post describing the genius of their creative machines. How can their methods be so straight-forward while we struggle with the basics? How do they attract and retain such creative talent while we struggle to build creative brand equity? And how can their leadership have such vision and their teams, such alignment?

These companies are shining examples of creativity because feelings of freedom and optimism shape their entire cultures. They can build the future because they can see that future clearly. With such vision, the leaders in these organizations are able to recruit and retain innovators and great thinkers. They have creative clarity.

But bringing the freedom of creativity into our own companies feels like adding to the crazy, not fixing it. Creative people are unpredictable and wild. They don't do well with our traditional management frameworks, and it often feels as though we can't manage them at all. We aren't much better at managing our creative processes. Some of our best tools, such as the design-thinking and lean methods, only scratch the surface of the business problems and the market threats we face. We don't have the organizational capacity to bring the mess into focus, so we flail and struggle.

It's time to *properly* drive an ethos of creativity into our companies. This is a new way of thinking about everything from process, to people, to organizational design—about building a company and a company culture that can see through the mess.

Creative clarity requires you to do four things:

1. Choreograph a creative strategy, describing a clear future even among the blurry business landscape.

2. Grow teams that include those creative, unpredictable outcasts; give them the space to produce amazing work; and build a unique form of trust in your company culture.

3. Institutionalize an iterative process of critique, conflict, and ideation.

4. Embrace chaos but manage creative spin and stagnation.

This book is primarily for people in charge of driving strategic change through an organization. If you are a line manager responsible for exploring a horizon of opportunity, the book will help you establish a culture of creative product development in which your teams can predictably deliver creative results. You'll learn methods to drive trust among your team members to enable you to critique and improve their work. And as an organizational leader, you'll complement your traditional business strategies with the new language and understanding you need to implement creativity in a strategic manner across your company.

In a creative environment, chaos is the backdrop for hidden wonderment and success. I want you to gain clarity in the face of that chaos, so you can build great products, great teams, and a high-performing creative organization.

WHAT TO EXPECT

Before we jump in, here's what you can expect to read and learn about.

CHAPTER 1: FRAMING PROBLEMS

Creative clarity starts with a crisp perspective of strategy. Your team members want a reason to believe in your company and in their own work—a reason that's bigger and more tangible than rewards of money or career progress. They're certainly looking for direction they can understand; but even more important is a vision they can *feel*. It's up to you to set that vision and help them see a tunnel of light through the murky business landscape. That doesn't mean you have to have the Big Idea or that the entire vision rests on your shoulders. It means you need to tell a story about an optimistic future and then help your team believe in that future. That story needs to be visual, and have depth; to bring creativity to life, traditional business platitudes won't cut it.

Walt Disney consistently used stories to communicate a new vision to his team. He even acted out those stories, as in the case of *Snow White and the Seven Dwarves*. He "...told the story of Snow White better than we put it on the screen....he portrayed all the parts....he became even the Queen, he became the Huntsman, he became the dwarves, he became Snow White." (Jones, 2013)

I'll help you build your story of the future, and you won't need to act it out. We'll craft a strategy and communicate a vision by framing persuasive and tangible creative opportunities and by producing artifacts that visualize the future.

To develop the story, you'll need to question or reject established opinions and look at things in new ways. This means *reframing*: purposefully shifting the presentation of a problem to bring new opportunities into focus.

In this chapter, I'll explain how framing and reframing works, and you'll hear from a former Senior Creative Director at Under Armour on the role of constraints in framing a problem. You'll learn—

1. *How to identify new framing boundaries through exploration.* Constraints emerge from the actual process of solving the problem. These new constraints cause the problem to flex, and when it does, new and unexpected ideas emerge.

2. *When and how to reject requirements.* Constraints act as containers for exploration. Requirements, on the other hand, act as though someone already knows the answer. The requirements to reject are the ones that prescribe not just what to do, but how to do it.

CHAPTER 2: BUILDING A CREATIVE STRATEGY

Creativity in businesses used to refer almost exclusively to the colors, layout, and collateral associated with advertising and product marketing. But modern creative strategy doesn't refer to the branding or packaging of your offering or to the marketing slogans used to present it. Creative strategy is a fundamental way of considering the value promise that a company makes to its customers. It's emotional as much as it is intellectual, and it's persuasive. In this chapter, I'll show you how to craft that creative strategy and give you a playbook for clarity. You'll explore the three components of this creative playbook—external forces, success criteria, and a north star—and learn how to make them work for you in your role. And, you'll learn how I used this creative strategy to launch a new generation of products when I was the Vice President of Design at Blackboard (the world's largest educational software companies).

CHAPTER 3: EXPLORING A PROBLEM SPACE

When we think of creativity, most of us imagine an artist like Jackson Pollack: alone in the studio and throwing paint all over a canvas. It seems like a mess, and a lot of it seems arbitrary.

It's neither of those things, and it doesn't add overhead or busywork. Creativity is actually a process that you can articulate and manage. It emphasizes *iteration*: the act of doing something over and over but with constant improvement, both to the idea and to its representation. Ideas start as fuzzy, poorly defined things; through iteration, they gain clarity and fidelity.

In addition to iteration, the creativity process sends ideas through *variation*—thinking sideways around a problem—to help move beyond the obvious to something unexpected and new. To explore a solution space (sometimes called the "muddy middle"), variation produces a quantity of ideas, rather than driving towards the best one.

You'll get a toolkit of methods to help you and your team work through iterations and variations. You'll learn to—

1. *Ignore constraints*. Temporarily explore beyond the confines of the

constraints, so you can work through ambiguity and add clarity. This work then establishes new constraints for further exploration.

2. *Isolate components.* Break a problem into experiential parts, and solve each part individually.

3. *Tell an end-to-end story.* To show how people will experience your new idea, restructure the parts in a narrative.

4. *Force a lateral provocation.* Leverage *what-if thinking*, driven by an external prompt, to explore an idea space in unexpected directions.

In this chapter, you'll also learn how a decade of iteration and variation led to BodyMedia's acquisition for $100M.

CHAPTER 4: MANAGING SPIN

Creativity feels like magic, where dreams come to life. Creative clarity demands a constant source of inspiration. It can be hard to be creative on demand, as the blank-canvas effect often rears its ugly head. Imagine a painter's canvas with nothing on it. That blankness can daunt an artist or a designer to whom any mark is a commitment.

The intimidation of those first steps can lead to a feeling of helplessness, which in turn can lead to using busywork to avoid the hard work. A treadmill of busywork brings exhaustion and more malaise—burnout. Even too much *creative* work can lead to burnout over time, as Author Scott Berkun describes: "The longer you work at creating things, whether it's websites, essays or paintings, the greater the odds you'll have [a] day where you don't feel like doing it anymore." (Berkun, 2004) At scale, that feeling can be toxic to your company.

Too much work and intimidation are not all that can be toxic to creativity and your company. The creative process is sensitive, and small things, such as distractions and unproductive criticism from the team itself or outside stakeholders, can have an unexpectedly large impact. As you communicate your teams' ideas to the organization, those ideas receive feedback: new knowledge, new opinions, and conflicting direction. The volume, intensity, and differing nature of this feedback can derail creativity and slow your progress.

The result of unstructured, unproductive, and contradictory feedback is *spin*: wasted creative cycles that don't push the idea forward. These cycles weigh heavily because they make a problem seem intractable. They cause designers to second- and third-guess their decisions and to fail to achieve the necessary state of flow. They cause timelines, budgets, and creative quality to suffer.

I'll show you the source of this unproductive criticism and arm you with the right language and tools to stop spin before it affects your team. You'll learn to block out the crowd to—

1. *Foster flow in your team.* Flow is the Zen-like state of productive, almost automatic work. To achieve flow, the team needs a clearly articulated goal, focused time to problem-solve, and a challenge that's "just hard enough."

2. *Minimize the ripple effect.* Your designers are focused on experience, so small changes at the beginning of an experience ripple through to the end. Bigger changes emit bigger ripples. Guarding against system changes saves time.

3. *Centralize the conversation around an artifact.* Ideas and thoughts tend to stray, and feedback is ambiguous. A creative conversation anchored on an artifact becomes actionable.

CHAPTER 5: RUNNING A CRITIQUE

The beginning of a creative engagement is called the "fuzzy front end" because it lacks clarity and structure. Developing new ideas in this phase is full of anxiety; when you and your business take creative risks, you may fail, and who wants to fail? As a natural reaction to that fear of risk, employees become skeptical of new ideas. In their concern that a given idea won't succeed, they poke, prod, and analyze every aspect of that untested idea. The more exciting the innovation, the more visibility it has within the company, and the more it seems to draw opinions—and worry—out of the woodwork. Those opinions are grounded in unstructured and unproductive debate. Worse, unsolicited opinions can cause unnecessary spin and build resentment among the team responsible for delivering the given product or service.

Critique, on the other hand, is a special type of feedback that identifies tactical issues, redirects a creative process as it steers off course, encourages sharing, and improves the quality of work. During a critique, a creative director and a team leverage patterns and prior knowledge to work through new explorations. They create a line of sight towards a better solution, driving through ambiguity towards clarity.

Critique is fundamental to a successful creative process. In this chapter, I'll show you how to run a critique session, focusing on these main principles:

1. *Critiquing the problem.* Require your teams to use "We promise to" value framing to articulate the problem they are solving and the reason they are solving it.

2. *Driving improvement.* While remaining constructive, steer conversation towards negative qualities of the current iteration, and explain why they are negative.

3. *Sketching in real time.* Draw alternative solutions during the critique, and help the team collaboratively understand the solution space.

CHAPTER 6: BUILDING A CREATIVE CULTURE

Any successful business culture is based on a fundamental of trust: Team members must believe they can depend on one another to do what's right. They must also believe the team is operating with the same mission and the best (shared) interests of the company in mind. In this chapter, I'll give you concrete ways to build trust with your team members so they can receive unedited and direct criticism about their artifacts without taking it personally.

You'll learn to—

1. *Build a culture of mentorship.* Your senior talent can develop your junior talent through an effective master-apprentice relationship. Mentorship builds trust without the dark side of formal titles and hierarchy.

2. *Identify creative ownership.* Establish an explicit design-product owner, and articulate that person's responsibility for creative output, craftsmanship, and delivery dates.

3. *Leverage passion projects.* Creative talent needs to unwind. Develop valuable team-building projects to recharge your team.

You'll hear from the former Chief Creative Officer of the company frog design about how to coach non-designers to give effective criticism when they lack a traditional creative vocabulary. And we'll explore trust through case studies from Earnest, a mid-stage financial-lending startup, and from the innovation lab at the U.S. Government's Office of Personnel Management.

CHAPTER 1

FRAMING PROBLEMS

THE ROLE OF VISION

Steve Jobs once said, "There needs to be someone who is sort of the keeper and reiterator of the vision. Because there is just a ton of work to do, and a lot of times when you have to walk a thousand miles and you take the first step, it looks like a long ways. And it really helps if there is someone there saying, 'well, we're one step closer. The goal definitely exists; it's not just a mirage out there.' So in a thousand and one little and sometimes larger ways, the vision needs to be reiterated. I do that a lot." (Bariso, n.d.)

Your creative team wants a reason to go to work, and as a creative leader, you need to provide the vision that Jobs describes. As an organization, we often spend time building mission and vision *statements*—short phrases that articulate the most high-level purpose of what we do. But without a *creative vision,* those statements often ring hollow or unbelievable.

The seeds of that creative vision often emerge from popular innovation frameworks, like lean's business canvas or design thinking's double diamond. These frameworks recommend that we suspend our skepticism of off-the-wall concepts so that we can move past incremental innovation to something groundbreaking. Coming up with these new ideas is like dreaming—we end with an idealized view of a new future. We imagine a new product or service in its best light because we view it optimistically. During the dream state of these innovation sessions, we imagine that our product is perfect and that we have the ability to deliver it. We tell stories of easier lives, a better world, and the financial benefits of a successful product-market fit.

For example, if we're working in an educational-software company, we might tell a story of how our new product (that doesn't yet exist) miraculously fixes the broken education system and makes our business successful. Imagine—

> Our product helps students identify their passions and find majors they love. By selecting a perfect course of study, they can learn a series of practical skills while simultaneously developing critical thinking. They'll graduate on time, and we'll help them find a great job they love.
>
> We capitalize on this value promise by selling our product to schools, and we become the market leader in this solution area. Because the product is so effective in driving retention outcomes, we can charge a premium justified by the near-term ROI for a given customer. We quickly become the central system for integrating disparate technology platforms, locking customers into a controlled ecosystem. We can grow multiple new products on the platform and leverage the data produced in aggregate to create and sell insights through consulting services.

The paragraph seems pretty great, as if we've tackled and fixed all of the seemingly impossible problems in education. This dreaming is useful because it anchors and motivates the team and helps to challenge the status quo. Visualizing the perfect state helps produce the direction for a team to move towards and align around. Without this vision, what my teams call the "Barbie Dream House," it's hard to identify correct decisions and measure success.

Because the vision assumes perfection, it is purposefully naïve. It forces us to temporarily ignore core-business realities. It doesn't need to account for budget constraints, technological limitations, political team dynamics, quarterly profits, time, and any of the other things that make a business a business.

But even while that idealized future motivates, the lack of realism can trigger anxious questions. How will we get there if we aren't properly equipped? How will we overcome the technical complexities of the vision? And if we don't have the right skills and capabilities, who will get us there?

It's tempting to try to answer these questions before knowing what that vision actually is. And it's hard to craft that vision when no clear boundaries exist yet to show us even *what problem we're solving*. To deal with the resulting anxiety, we often try to minimize risk: We back away from the beauty and perfection of the new idea. Our overly idealized future solves a problem, but because we aren't sure it's the right problem, we limit ourselves.

To feel that we are solving the right problem, we need a way to give the problem *form*.

Creative constraints are the way to frame the problem space, allow for exploration, and bring an idealized vision of the future into a more practical, approachable reality. Constraints form a container around an idea so we can move it from idealistic towards realistic. That container acts as a set of rules. Although you might think of rules as stifling, they aren't. In fact, the process of making things *flourishes* within creative constraints. For creative people in particular, constraints are one of the most valuable thinking tools.

Creative constraints support innovation for two reasons. First, unlike requirements, constraints are flexible. They can shift as innovations push the boundaries of traditional "appropriate" thinking, and as they shift, the creative process can follow. Second, constraints often emerge from the creative exploration itself. That means the creative team has ownership over the boundaries, not just the solution.

We've all had the "Aha!" experience while we work through a problem: We suddenly see the problem clearly from a new perspective. Constraints emerge from these mini moments. We create them during the creative process, leverage them during exploration, and evolve or abandon them as the fidelity and detail of an idea changes. And when you look at that elusive question—"what are we building?," constraints start to point to answers. They provide a way to say "this, but not that"; they provide the product *framing*.

UNDERSTANDING FRAMING

Framing describes the perspective you take during any situation. The cognitive-psychology theory of framing states that people interpret their experiences through a lens informed by their life experiences. This happens naturally and continuously—it's how we make sense of the world. The trouble is that, while any particular frame reveals new and interesting content, it also serves to conceal some information. With any given frame, we may miss an opportunity that might have been obvious if we had looked through a different frame. Think of this as a perspective bias: We always have a one-sided view of a situation based on the lens we choose.

We typically think of a bias as a bad thing. But once we understand how framing works, we can use perspective bias to our advantage. We can become more aware of our active frame by considering the assumptions we are making about a given event, experience, action, or activity. And that awareness allows us to shift around the frame. We can even *reframe a situation*, to view it from another perspective.

Let's come back to our higher-education example. Are you reading in the news about the inflated costs of academia and getting more and more worked up about poor graduation rates and sky-high student debt? It's easy to be the armchair quarterback: Why don't they just get better teachers? Why don't they just lower the cost of tuition? Why don't the students just work harder?

Now imagine that situation from the perspective of the academic deans who have to manage decreasing budgets under more and more scrutiny. Instead of judging these deans, try to visualize the situation from their point of view: Consider what their perspective on life might be, why they have their job, what motivates them to work every morning, what they think of you, what they think of the policies they have to follow, and so on.

Now imagine a student, taking a test in a required sophomore chemistry class, and the other people involved in the experience: the proctor, who administers the exam; the teacher's assistant, who helped to prepare the student for the test; the instructor, who taught the student, developed the curriculum and the test, and who will grade the test. If you shift your frame of reference, you zoom out from the topic to see a relationship even to the parents, the academic dean, and potential employers. All of these people are looking at an objective reality: a student took a test in a specific way.

Because we don't have the benefit of omniscience, our perspective is shaped by the emotional impact and contextual information we have about the experience. If the student does poorly but had attended office hours, the instructor may empathize and be more lenient on grading that exam. The parent may direct frustration over a poor score into anger at the student. And that same score might demoralize the student enough to drop the class.

Each participant in the objective event has a subjective view of it, often limited by individual experience. In each case, that view puts a box, built from past experience and personal knowledge, around what really happened. The box acts as the initial *constraints of understanding*.

Additionally, each participant views that event and subsequent events through a lens that distorts reality. That distorted lens so dramatically influences what we think happened that it *becomes a new reality*, at least for that participant.

FRAMING IN PROBLEM SOLVING

When confronted with a new creative problem, creative teams have learned that the initial boundary conditions are rarely the real rules of the road. They're only the first frame. So to establish a larger and richer idea space, the teams have also learned to reframe a problem to view these conditions through as many lenses as possible.

Articulating these boundary conditions and lenses fosters creativity. After marinating in the mess of constraints, we'll synthesize the boundary conditions into a single framing statement.

As we work our way towards creative clarity, we'll use a specific case as an example of each artifact, method, and technique presented. We'll ground the work in a fictional educational software company called **Succeed!** that's entering the market with a new product offering. You'll get to play CEO, creative director, and designer all at once, and you'll see how the different methods work at different levels of problem abstraction.

> We're in our product-kickoff meeting. As the CEO, customers (primarily school superintendents and principals) tell you over and over that students aren't prepared to succeed in college. You've reflected on this statement, and in meetings and in conference calls within your company, you've been trying on the phrase "student success." This idea emerges as the first problem frame: **an opportunity exists to help students succeed in their journey from high school to college.** Although that statement frames the problem at a high level of abstraction, it forms some of the initial constraints for creative problem solving. Look at all it encapsulates:
>
> 1. We're creating something for students.
>
> 2. We're creating something to help students transition from high school to college.
>
> 3. We're creating something for people who go to college.
>
> 4. We're creating something for **success**, although we haven't defined success yet.
>
> Let's explore product framing from the perspective of a given person, rather than a product landscape. Consider the map of all of the people whom our yet-to-be-created product could positively influence along with their perspectives, wants, and needs:

Person	Emotional characterization	Implications of that perspective	Framing statement
Students	nervous, anxious, expectant	will make haphazard choices, and will make them quickly will feel lost, and will look for guidance will feel embarrassed, and may avoid asking explicitly for help won't know how to best present themselves in their best light	We are designing new features in our homework product to help students gain enough confidence to make informed decisions about their future.
Instructors	optimistic in general, but somewhat resigned to the fact that not everyone will succeed	will support motivated students in a college search will feel a sense of hopelessness about some of the less-successful students will feel they don't have enough time to help every student individually	We are designing a new product to give instructors the time to help all students plan for the future.
Guidance Counselors	committed to success, but frustrated with the mechanized system of college admissions; overwhelmed by the quantity of students requiring help	will try to provide individualized attention to each student will leverage formula-style approaches that have proven to be successful	We are designing a new suite of products to find out about students' aspirations and help guidance counselors create individualized plans for each student.
Parents	overwhelmed by choices	will be confused, and may give up quickly will leverage anecdotal feedback or advice from friends and family	We are designing a new product to help parents narrow college choices to just a few.
Admissions Officers	overwhelmed by candidates and incoming questions from parents	will try to down-select students as quickly as possible to get to a manageable subset of candidates are worried that their decisions don't account for ethnicity, gender, and socioeconomic status	We are designing a new product to help admissions officers make fairer decisions.

and more…

We're identifying all four columns—the people, their emotional characterization, the implications of those emotions, and the frame itself—based on our own knowledge and experience. Design thinking enables customer research that helps us build empathy with audiences as it shapes our understanding of various frames. That type of research acts as a sort of hedge, so we can be more confident in the types of generalizations we make.

The "implications" column is the most important. It predicts behavior and starts to address how someone will respond to a new idea, product, or service. It's also the biggest leap from our own point of reference because it demands that we jump out of our comfort zone. Once you establish implications, the frame naturally follows.

Notice how the frame now makes judgment easier. It's easy to look at creative solutions and say, "yes, this does that" or "no, this **doesn't** do that."

We're just at the beginning of the creative process, but each initial frame we select at this stage will color what we do next. The framing statement creates a starting point for creative exploration, for user research, for market sizing, and for business model canvassing.

The initial frame can't be *wrong* because it's shaped by each team members' perspective. We automatically start with a frame built on our own experiences, remembering what it was like to be a student, or leveraging conversations we had with our child's teachers. But because our perspective is unique, the initial frame is the first opportunity for *misalignment* in our team. Each team member's unique frame of reference leads to a different view of the problem being solved. That means initial, and subsequent moves will probably go in different directions. It's critical that the team is aware of the selected frame and that it realigns around a purposeful reframing of the problem.

WRITE EACH ACTIVE FRAME, IN LARGE LETTERS, WHERE THE TEAM CAN SEE IT. REWRITE IT EACH TIME IT CHANGES. TO DERIVE IMPLICATIONS AND EMOTIONAL CHARACTERIZATIONS, WORK THROUGH ALL POTENTIAL FRAMES.

USING PROBLEM FRAMING AND CONSTRAINTS
TO SHIFT CORPORATE STRATEGY

For any organization that plans a major redirection, framing the problem and establishing constraints are critical to achieving alignment. The evolution of Under Armour (UA) illustrates those truths. Traditionally a (massively successful) retailer of its branded sports clothing and gear, UA decided to shift toward digital after making over $710 million in digital acquisitions.

Digital is different, though; it means embracing fast iteration, launching incomplete products, and engaging in different forms of product marketing and distribution models. The company didn't know how to craft and launch digital products.

The two main challenges looked like this—

- *Tactical:* Integrate new digital capabilities into a single platform, so that customers can benefit from the features of each product.

- *Strategic:* Transform an apparel company into a software company that leverages technology to improve athletic performance. (This type of challenge is increasingly common as other established companies grapple with how to change their product-development methods to account for the strange way software comes to life.)

They were particularly challenging for two reasons:

- *Different capabilities.* Many of UA's employees are experts in bringing soft goods (such as socks and shorts) to market. That includes understanding the products' nuances: seasonal shifts, long development lead times, physical-product manufacturing, merchandising, and channel partnerships. Those staff members are *not* experts in digital technology. As recently as three years before,

CEO Kevin Plank explains, the company's digital strategy had "consisted of a single website." (Trites, n.d.)

- *Different opinions.* As is typical, not everyone in the company was on board with the change. Against a landscape of success—UA's stock had jumped from 13.20 to more than 100 in just five years—a billion-dollar investment in digital was bound to draw critics. Employees asked themselves, "If we're so successful doing what we've always done, why change?" Questions also came from outside. Morningstar Retail Analyst Paul Swinand described the change as a massive and risky bet: " ...when you're hitting a home run every quarter on the core apparel business, why mess around with a moon shot?" (Foster, 2016).

But the executive leadership activated the "moon shot," which meant developing not just digital products but an entire digital organization. The change would require strategic alignment around not just *what to build* but also *how to build it.*

That's where framing came in. The CEO produced the first frame, a strategic one that helped to articulate the problem as organizational alignment. The frame positioned the problem of technology around the emotions of health and the choices related to fitness: "*We are designing a new organization to help people make better health decisions.*" Along with resources contributed by the company's acquisitions, this problem frame also—

- provided the knowledge and the people to build a plan around technology,

- suggested that technology is about helping people feel better and make better health decisions, not about cool websites or even advanced performance materials,

- leveraged the collective experience of the company in supporting health and wellness,

- attempted to see the world through the eyes of athletes, and

- was deliberately vague and fuzzy, while offering a vision for the future that rallied the team.

Evan Torchin was a Creative Director (with UA's "Connected Fitness" platform) at the center of the corporate strategy shift. To act as liaison between people and products and to fine-tune the frame, Torchin says he established constraints—which he calls "guardrails"—around the problem. It takes time to frame a problem correctly, he says; if you haven't, "You will spin forever...." To get it right, he advises doing the work to frame a problem "based in inputs from all sorts of sources; whether it's consumer insights, or gut; whether it's based on assessment of the market, or real market data...." (Torchin, 2016)

Although the CEO produced the initial frame, it was important that the constraints did not come from the top, say Torchin and Paul Pugh, former

VP of Connected Fitness. Constraints emerged instead from staff perspectives, market data, creative exploration, gut instinct, and ultimately through the creative process itself.

Torchin further describes the constraints' critical role in rallying other people in the organization around a single goal. Guardrails, he says, build consensus by providing "a framework for talking about a feature or service or concept."

Through iteration, Torchin's product team shifted the CEO's initial framing toward a focus on *experience of use*. The reframe states, *"We are designing a new set of interconnected products that have a seamless, end-to-end work-flow."* As it sounds, that frame emerged, not from typical constraints such as market landscape or a competitive feature set, but from the constraints of using the products. For example, with Bluetooth, "…often just connecting a single device can be a pain." The framing around "experience of use," then, turned troubleshooting features that are usually afterthoughts into early and fundamental design concerns.

Why couldn't the product team members just start with that frame? The reason is that they must be the *shepherds* of an emergent product vision, never its *source*. The tricky role of inspiring confidence in a direction without prescribing a solution belongs solely to the executive leadership.

The product team extracted the reframe through exploration in the face of that ambiguity. Creative people tend to tolerate it far more easily than analytical ones do. In fact, ambiguity can drive the analytical crazy; it can be scary to take on a problem without knowing where it's going. But the absence of a top-down mandate means the absence of a right path to follow. It also demands trust and comfort with even more ambiguity: Until the creative process is firmed up, the product-management and -launch teams, as well as channel partners and customers, need to be okay without answers to questions like, "what features will be available?" and "when will they be available?"

Let's turn our attention to how a creative strategy emerges from this framing and these constraints.

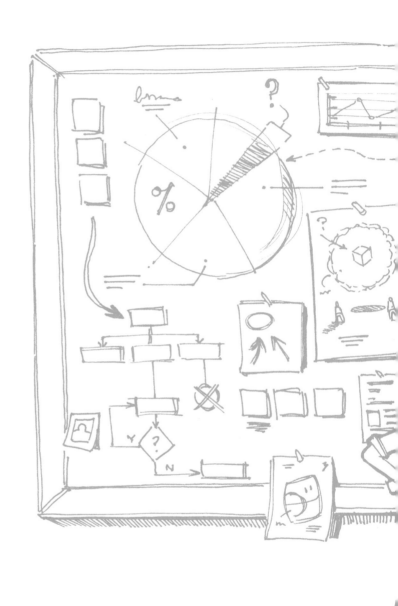

Talking about strategy is hard, so it often goes unstated. It exists in many companies as only a cultural feeling, and that can frustrate the people who have to do the heavy lifting. They don't know where they are going, unless it's in many directions at once.

But by *articulating* the strategy, a team can better rally around it and more effectively contribute to it. First, let's call it a *creative* strategy because we are creating something. Creativity in this context refers to a way of thinking about experience, not about aesthetics, color, and composition. It refers to *how we'll solve a problem.*

A creative strategy includes these core components:

1. *External forces.* Shaping the starting point for exploration, these inputs are qualitative ethnographic (user) research, market-dynamic signals, engineering limitations, and stakeholder opinions.

2. *Success criteria* in the form of creative guidelines.

3. *North star and value proposition.* The north star tells us where to go, while the value proposition describes the promise made to customers even before the creative work has started.

Let's look at each idea in more depth.

EXTERNAL FORCES

When we begin to develop a creative strategy, the external inputs that *should* come together into a synthesized whole are often misaligned. Sometimes leadership articulates these inputs, and they trickle down through the company. Sometimes they emerge bottom-up; customer research often drives them. These customer dynamics often take the form of stories. They include direct quotes and observations from real people. They articulate wants and needs. They shape a strategy grounded in reality. These inputs help to shape the initial problem frames, and by leveraging what people say and do, each constraint is grounded in empathy.

To define this part of your creative strategy, first articulate the inputs that come top-down in a more autocratic fashion.

Back at our fictional company **Succeed!** we're beginning to build our creative strategy. We've identified problem framing around students. Our overall framing statement began as, **An opportunity exists to help students succeed in their journey from high school to college**, describing a strategy synthesized from customer visits and from an external view of the market.

That statement evolved to focus on the application process itself and students' support networks, like guidance counselors and parents. The revised statement is, **An opportunity exists to help students apply to college with the support they need to make informed and confident decisions.**

Now we'll write a brief that describes the creative strategy. With the revised framing statement in mind, consider these real-world mandates from various stakeholders.

› The VP of sales, responsible for selling our existing k12 applications, feels that we must add new capabilities that help students showcase their best work. This will help us remain competitive with other homework and admissions apps we often lose to when we go to market.

› As the CEO, you know that we're contemplating a deal with a third-party portfolio tool, so our new features may need to leverage their APIs.

These are the *top-down* external influencers. They can be challenging, as they pre-suppose both problems and solutions. One person's knowledge and experience often form them, so they aren't necessarily wrong. But because they don't leave room for customer or user input, creative expression, or constraints development, they also aren't necessarily right.

Articulate these top-down stakeholder opinions by focusing on quotes from stakeholders. What attributable quotes can you use to present how each team leader feels about the product or features?

> "I'm just seeing a ton of momentum in the portfolio space. Increasingly, students need to apply to college with work samples."
> **–Product marketing lead**

> "We really need to consider options related to build, buy, and integrate. I have a contact at a third-party company who is willing to cut us a deal." **–Director of third-party partnerships**

These quotes describe new ways of thinking about the problem, new lenses to apply on an otherwise blank space. They are rarely prescriptive; they don't tell you what to build. Instead, they add structure to the problem. Articulating them doesn't commit you to *doing* these things, but you are starting to map out a sandbox for exploration. Also, the very act of articulating them can build support and consensus. These quotes show that you heard someone and internalized what they had to say. Torchin, the UA Creative Director, describes the quotes as showing, "… It's a company effort. It's not like you are forcing your way in, kicking a door; someone above you believes in that vision as well."

Next, move on to internally perceived technical constraints. Describe the things that your engineering and technical teams view as limitations on what you can accomplish.

> There's no way to integrate with all third-party college-application

systems. We'll have to pick the market leader and focus on integrating with that.

We don't have an established way to save rich media, like photos and videos; we have no data store for student-specific content other than grades.

It will take way too long to process video uploads at scale.

Describing his framing process at UA, Torchin explains, "You want to understand the technology being used by your engineers, so you aren't designing something impossible or (that) would take two years to build and that no one wants to invest in." Again, these are perceptions, not requirements. But those perceptions matter: The employees who will be doing the implementing have to believe they *can* do it. That means they need to be invested in the proposed pathway towards a solution.

Describe external market forces. Paint a picture of the competitive and emergent market landscape without fixating on a single competitive product.

Because of the increasing connection between assessment and evidence-based learning, students are emerging from high school with a portfolio of completed work.

College admissions officers are overwhelmed by the sheer number of applications and need a way to rapidly move through and evaluate them.

Grades are only one of the pieces students use to apply to school. They also leverage their extra-curricular activities, letters of recommendation, and even—for some international students—letters that prove the ability to pay for school.

These ideas are externally focused but synthesized from a variety of sources. To shape these statements, you'll need a picture of the historic problem landscape. This is called *tacit knowledge*. By definition, *tacit knowledge* is difficult to describe (it represents things you know so intimately that you don't necessarily know you know them). So you'll need to work to articulate this knowledge in a way the team can understand.

Leverage end-user quotes and behavioral observations. These are some of the most important constraints. Quotes and observations from real people ground further exploration in an empathetic perspective of pain points.

> "I don't really have anything to showcase about the skills I learned in school. I didn't do any sports; mostly I'm good at video games."

> "I try to help all of the students prepare for school, but the reality is that I have 140 juniors applying to school and close to the same amount who aren't even looking. I can't help them all, and I end up helping only the ones that are proactive—the students that need my help the least."

> "We want our son to go to school, but we just can't afford it. I know there are financial aid packages available, but I don't know how to apply and we just don't have time."

You can see the power of these quotes—they probably made you start thinking of solutions. These quotes come from observing behavior. They often describe the aspirations, hope, dreams, concerns, perceptions, and fears of the people who will benefit most from the products you build. These are the most important guardrails because they shape unexpected constraints, the boundaries that often extend the furthest outside of your comfort zone. And most important, they indicate *latent needs*—customer needs that lie below the surface, waiting to be fulfilled. This is innovation opportunity, the places where creativity can best drive market disruption.

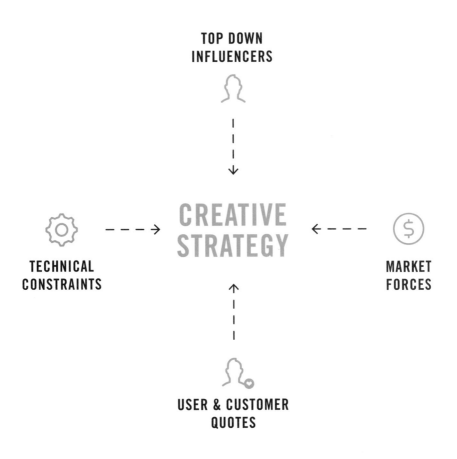

TOP DOWN
INFLUENCERS

CREATIVE
STRATEGY

TECHNICAL
CONSTRAINTS

MARKET
FORCES

USER & CUSTOMER
QUOTES

Reflect on the content of our creative strategy so far.

1. We articulated top-down influencers, those mandates coming from influential people in our organization.

2. We identified technical, real-world boundaries that limit what we can do and how we can do it.

3. We discussed external market forces in an attempt to make tacit knowledge explicit.

4. We identified the most important end-user and customer quotes.

These items don't solve the problem. Instead, they identified the *shape* of the problem.

Let's return to the phrase, *the shape of the problem:* It captures how elusive creative problems can be when you first start. A well-defined problem has boundaries you can articulate, creating a clear, crisp shape. An ill-defined problem, on the other hand, lacks boundaries, so its shape is amorphous and fuzzy. As we build the creative strategy, we're making that fuzzy problem into something more crisp and well defined.

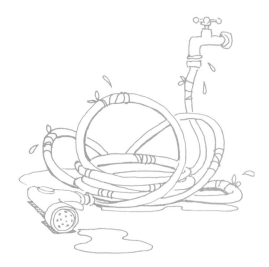

WRITE DOWN INFLUENCERS, BOUNDARIES, MARKET FORCES, AND CUSTOMER INSIGHTS.

SUCCESS CRITERIA

Success criteria take the form of creative constraints. It is rare that constraints of any substantive value are mandated top-down on the creative team. Sure, we listed top-down influencers before, and your team will have to work within real time limits, financial boundaries, and other top-down realities of business. But the most valuable type of creative constraints are those that come from an intimacy with the content and subject matter; they emerge through a back-and-forth process of making and thinking—from a sort of conversation with the *thing being made*.

When the *thing being made* is...

- ...a physical object, the main constraints are also physical: the materials and their cost, manufacturing abilities, sourcing mechanisms, and competitive landscape of features and functions.

- ...a qualitative-research study with real people, the main constraints emerge from the selection criteria: whom to study and what you will observe.

- ... a new product or application, constraints typically emerge from the process of storytelling: creating use cases, scenarios, and storyboards that show a person using a hypothetical product to achieve a goal.

- ... a corporate strategy, the main constraints often come from a leader with a strong vision of the future.

Design Theorist Henrik Gedenryd describes that the rigidity of constraints depends on whether they are mandated ("legislated," in Gedenryd's words) or more organically emergent. An architect designing a building would never set out to build a dangerous one, but setting an intention about safety isn't enough. Instead, explicit constraints come in the form of a building code that potentially limits the architect's ability for exploration. These constraints are non-negotiable, even as the creative process acts as a form of what Gedenryd calls *material negotiation.*

But constraints that emerge from the work itself are only temporarily strict and rigid. They can be applied absolutely but for only a short time. The creative team can establish parameters to essentially overrule creative directions to arrive at a manageable solution set. When those solutions aren't very good, the very team that created them has complete control to flex the constraints and develop new ones. (Gedenryd, 1998)

All of that theory has practical implications, as well. The distinction between mandated and emergent constraints is an important one. The product owner or a technologist can't set the constraints that emerge from the work because, until the creative process happens, they don't yet exist.

The mandated constraints are more traditional requirements. Typically, these requirements are gathered through an internal perspective on what the market will bear, combined with an engineering perspective on what is possible. These requirements are the initial guardrails that Torchin described and the boundaries that Gedenryd calls "non-negotiable."

When the initial guardrails jibe with the emergent guardrails, and when the non-negotiable requirements are in harmony with the emergent ones, creativity flourishes. Misalignment and friction occurs when the top-down and bottom-up perspectives are at odds. The creative team then sees the requirements as stifling, as if a checklist can bind creativity. But no one likes being told what to do, and creative teams are particularly finicky about creative exploration. So as you build your creative strategy, minimize requirements and maximize the opportunity for emergent design constraints.

Here are some of the similarities and differences between constraints and requirements.

Creative Constraints	Requirements
Emerge "bottom up" through the creative process itself	Are provided "top down": Stakeholders prescribe them
Can change through the creative process	Are fixed
The creative team "owns" them	The business "owns" them
Encourage creativity	Limit creativity
Take the form of *"The product must"* and *"the user will have the ability to"*	Take the form of *"The product must"* and *"the user will have the ability to"*
Help contain the creative space to make it more manageable	Help contain the creative space to make it more manageable
Act as criteria for judging success	Act as criteria for judging success

Constraints are often described as *the product must* statements and *the user will have the ability to* statements.

The product must be free for parents and students to use and download; we must find an external source to monetize.

The product's go-to-market strategy must support symbiotic partnerships with other college-prep solutions and offerings.

The product's content must be sourced from a partner that has credibility within academic administrative circles.

Students will have the ability to describe themselves in language they understand.

Students will have the ability to identify financial aid benefits that they are eligible for.

Students will have the ability to one-click-apply to college.

You may find yourself with what seems like hundreds of these types of constraints. That's fine; what's important is to remain at two levels of description and fidelity at once. First, make each *individual* constraint explicit, even if the designer established it during the creative process. Making constraints explicit enables objective judgment ("You said it would do that, but it doesn't") and further exploration points ("We said we would have a joint partnership with a trusted content provider; who is in charge of working that deal and building that relationship?")

Next, form constraints into categories, described in a way that a busy team member can quickly understand. Many *ability to* statements can roll up into larger container statements ("Ability to manage finances" or "Ability to represent themselves"). These group statements act as anchors for alignment. When a team comes together, its members need to trust that they are pursuing the same goals as they were during the last review. These grouping statements point a trajectory or course—and become ways to make sure the bus is going in the right direction.

So far, we've listed external forces and identified the constraints that point towards success criteria. A third type of constraint shapes the experience of the new product or service. These are statements that describe *how the solution should feel* without describing what it *should be*. They are *experience* principles, which might include thinking about usability, appeal, or engagement. Although these constraints don't have to be quantitative, they can be tracked and judged.

Experience principles are often reactive because they describe aspects of a solution that are different and better than a current solution.

> Our design will **feel collaborative**, helping students feel as though they are not alone.

Our design will **feel like an individual mentor** to a student.

Our design will **feel personal,** so students feel unique.

The team can establish metrics related to each principle, and, once a solution exists and reaches pilot or test phase, the team can assess whether they've made progress on these fronts. These metrics can emerge almost naturally from the external inputs.

It's really tempting at this part of the process to try to create solutions to the problems we've seen from customers and users, and from the competitive market landscape. But we're not ready for that because we haven't yet clearly articulated the problem. Don't abandon those solutions, though. Write them down and park them. You can come back to them when you start building things.

DISCOVER CONSTRAINTS THROUGH EXPLORATION, INSTEAD OF MANDATING REQUIREMENTS UPFRONT.

NORTH STAR AND VALUE PROPOSITION

Now that you've articulated the external inputs and the design constraints, you can author the single most important part of the creative strategy: the summary problem statement. This statement encapsulates the vision for the product, service, or experience we'll build; it's the mission statement, including three core elements: *We are designing*, *We are designing for*, and *We promise to*.

The *we are designing* statement explains what we will strive to build over the timeframe of the project. The *we are designing for* part articulates who benefits from the new product or service. And the *we promise to* statement acts as a grounding anchor for a value proposition.

This problem statement becomes the main frame, the main point of alignment, and—when it's not referenced and honed—the main point of conflict for the team. For our college-admissions example, it looks like this:

> **We are designing** a tool to help students apply to the right college with the right financial aid package.

The statement makes clear that we aren't designing a course registration system, a homework-help system, a textbook sales system, or any of the other thousands of possibilities; it immediately focuses on one area. If we stopped here, our teams would at least be able to focus. We don't need to pursue a joint partnership with a tutoring company because we aren't offering tutoring services. But meeting with a potential customer who's a big college lender, seems like a good use of time.

Of course, the statement leaves a huge amount of vague whitespace in it, which is why we also described the target audience—whom *we are designing for:*

We are designing a tool to help students apply to the right college with the right financial aid package. **We are designing for** three audiences:

› Students, so they can better succeed in their academic journey,

› Parents, so they can make more informed decisions, and

› Guidance counselors, so they can better manage their limited time and resources.

Each pairing includes the persona (students, parents, and guidance counselors) and the goal for each persona (succeed in an academic journey, make informed decisions, manage limited time and resources). *Now* we have a view of the goals people will try to achieve with the not-yet-designed product.

These persona/goal pairings lead to even more detail in the form of a value promise for each persona:

We promise to:

› Help students build financial-aid packages with ease, find a school where they will be successful, and apply to that school.

› Help parents better understand the college-admissions process, better prepare for the financial burden of college, and support their student in the logistics of a college application (on time, correctly filled out, etc.).

› Help guidance counselors identify the status of each student's application, spread their knowledge to a larger audience, and personally help students who need help the most.

We are essentially saying "we promise we will do these things, and if we don't do them, we've failed you." These promises also speak to initial features and functions: For example, now we know the system will need to—

- source data related to financial aid and schools,

- manage lists of students,

- track application status, and

- integrate with admissions software at the university...

PUTTING IT ALL TOGETHER

We've discussed a creative strategy that contains external forces, success criteria, north star and value proposition. The documentation of this strategy acts as a flexible single source of truth; it holds many of the keys to managing a subjective and messy creative process. The team bases its creative exploration on constraints articulated in the strategy document. When the exploration brings up new constraints and creative paths, as it will, the document reflects and seeks to explain them.

Constraints that describe the user experience serve as emotional checks against actual design work. They encourage the designer to create delightful experiences, not just to architect features and functions. By documenting external inputs, you can ensure that each function has been heard and is represented in the new product development *without* your feeling as though you are serving a hundred masters. The problem statement itself becomes the north star, at least until a more robust creative representation, like a prototype, replaces it.

Strategy documentation also acts as a sort of next-step guide for other activities. Based on the constraints, a team may need to negotiate a data-sourcing partnership with a third party. Based on a capability described as an *ability to*, the engineering team may need to, say, research API integration with a separate internal system. The documented items each unlock—in an aligned manner—things to do and people to do them.

Making and sharing a document with this content means that the team has successfully framed the problem. The team can now make things with the confidence that they are solving the right problem.

DESCRIBE THE VALUE PROMISE AS A PROMISE OF BENEFIT.

AN EMERGENT CREATIVE STRATEGY

Let's take a look at how this form of creative strategy came together for Blackboard, the largest educational-software company in the world. Founded in 1997, the company invented a product category called "learning management systems," tools for students and teachers. Students use the tools to participate in online discussions and share homework and other documents. Teachers use them to grade assignments, provide feedback, and hold online classes.

After years of dramatic organic growth (new product development) and inorganic growth (acquisitions), the company fell directly into the trap of the innovator's dilemma. Market share and revenue sagged when competitors launched products that had fewer features but were perceived as easier to use. In an attempt to slow the decline, the company acquired a number of companies.

Simultaneously, the educational landscape began to experience two shifts. First, students have become increasingly focused on vocational job placement. They look at academic programs now as career gateways; they expect a return on their investment. Schools, in turn, have followed students' lead. They have shifted curricula from just transferring knowledge toward teaching skills that employers want.

Next, rising tuitions forced students to make non-traditional educational decisions. Students have become consumers, making more personalized decisions about how to spend their tuition. For example, they might attend more than one school at a time, put their education on hold midway through, transfer from school to school, take night classes, or build a hybrid educational plan.

To spark innovation and a strategic shift toward a focus on students, Blackboard made a successful acquisition move in 2014 by buying MyEdu. This startup helped students to succeed in college, tell their personal story of growth, and get a job soon after graduating.

The explanation of Jay Bhatt, Blackboard's CEO at the time of the acquisition, set forth his vision of the future: "We are…implementing a new business strategy that is keenly focused on providing more value to our end users—students. Adding MyEdu to our portfolio helps them solve two major challenges: graduating on time and securing a job." (Shah, 2014) This statement was the first reframe of the problem space: moving from the pragmatics of delivering content in the classroom to the larger problems of graduation completion and follow-up. It's also the first articulation of a creative strategy because it hints at *We are designing, We are designing for,* and *We promise to.*

Before the acquisition, the MyEdu product team took a creative approach to problem framing grounded in research. The team looked to students to better understand the problem space and to frame a value proposition, rather than focus on market shifts and trends. This research took the form of *ethnography*—spending time with students in their dorm rooms to identify their wants, needs, and habits. For example, the team learned that students take courses out of sequence or courses that don't count towards their major, which leads to unhappiness and attrition. The team also learned that as students begin to think about post-graduation employment, they struggle to form a strong representation of self.

Soon after the acquisition, the team at Blackboard developed a creative problem assertion: *We want students to feel confident in making decisions, while aware that change is not to be feared.* (Kolko, 2016) This assertion acted as creative framing of value, much like the guardrails that Torchin described at Under Armour. It contains a problem space, providing a scaffold for exploration. It also acts as criteria for judging ideas; a good idea supports that problem assertion, while a bad idea ignores or rejects the assertion.

The assertion led the start of a cultural shift: It helped to shift Blackboard away from a more traditional focus on the pragmatics of teaching and learning towards an emphasis on students and their decisions. The product team then synthesized the hundreds of research hours into a series of core insights that could drive product development and ultimately influence business strategy.

The core insights—

- Students have no mental model of the long-term financial consequences of short-term lifestyle decisions. They make irresponsible and uninformed spending decisions that they later regret.

- Students view their academic journey as a linear path; they start thinking about their job prospects only when it is too late to make important changes to their course of study.

- Because students aren't aware of their passions and interests, they don't see a connection between their developing skills and a fulfilled life. As a result, they lose interest in their courses of study and either change majors or drop out of school entirely.

- Students seeking an empathetic voice to help guide them on their journey receive only general guidance from overloaded advisors. Without more personalized and specific support, they feel isolated, alone, and unsupported.

- Students have difficulty planning their courses. They fail to register in time or take courses out of sequence or that don't count for credit, resulting in high anxiety, poor performance, and attrition. (Kolko, 2016)

The preliminary manifestation of this new way of thinking about academia was in a lab experiment called Job Genie. The experiment provided an opportunity to see how the organization itself responded to a new product strategy.

The team developed the product itself to explore the relationship between students' *self-discovery and job exploration.* The team hypothesized that beyond students' struggle to articulate their skills and interests, many feel that they don't have any skills at all. In Job Genie, students identify their aspirations in language they understand (power, money, impact), and then receive recommendations of different career options. The tool was experiential, not goal directed; rather than pointing students to a particular path towards a job, it let them explore linkages among jobs.

The product vignette succeeded, in that it acted as both a catalyst for change (of both framing and culture) and as framing criteria manifested as reality: The product began to steer the ship, tilting it ever so slightly in a new direction.

Soon after launching Job Genie, Blackboard developed Blackboard Planner (Bb Planner), a tool to address colleges' attrition and retention challenges. Leveraging MyEdu's tactical capabilities, the team combined the learnings from Job Genie and actual university data to create a more specific and valuable product.

Blackboard Planner combines the exploratory, experiential part of self-discovery with specific courses of study. Students can learn a little about themselves through introspection, find out about a particular career path, and identify majors at their school that lead in that direction. The product checks in with students to see how they are feeling. It shows them their progress towards completing a major and the amount of time it would take to attain a credential that steers them in the right direction.

Along the way, students encounter academic planning tools like those in MyEdu, financial planning tools, and opportunities to engage with alumni in a mentorship capacity. And their major and course choices are consistently presented in the context of job opportunities.

Each of these evolutions act as glimpses of an evolving creative strategy on value:

- With MyEdu, the company set out to solve the problem of personal identity by helping college students to tell their personal stories. This acquisition indicated a financial investment in student-centric innovation.

- With Job Genie, the company set out to solve the problem of helping college students to learn about career paths. This initiative showed organic innovation, further identifying students as the primary focus of a product strategy.

- Blackboard Planner's goal was to help students with planning a course of study focused on graduation—taking the right classes at the right time. This tool solidified the shift in thinking away from enterprise software for academia and towards consumer software for students.

Over the course of three years, Blackboard has been able to reframe the entire problem space at a strategic level, which then translated into new problems to solve at a tactical product level. First, the company shifted to student-centric by describing the strategic business problem around *employ-*

ment for graduates. Next, the company positioned the problem around *student decision-making,* focusing on how a student responds to the demands of the academic journey. Finally, the company launched Bb Planner by reframing the problem around *student success*; the new product relates to the other solutions while acting as an innovation in the new opportunity space.

The different perspectives aren't pivots—no one change is a wholesale shift in the company strategy, nor does it represent a moment of defeat or failure in an existing strategy. Instead, each is a lens on a problem space, emerging through slow change. The lenses act as those guardrails for creativity, as well as tools for organizational alignment. (Kolko, 2016)

For the team at Blackboard, value definition occurred at a number of conceptual levels:

CORPORATE STRATEGY
OUR VISION OF THE FUTURE

PRODUCT ITERATIONS
OUR VALUE OFFERINGS

PRODUCT CAPABILITIES
OUR DELIVERY MECHANISM FOR VALUE

First, exploring value at a corporate level helped steer the entire company towards new business lines. This was a vision of the future, a persuasive story of how the world might be. Blackboard leveraged acquisitions to jumpstart that creative shift, and articulate to the market that the company was entering the next phase in their value proposition.

Next, iterations at a product level created innovations with new audiences and steered decision making around a theme. Blackboard launched new products that integrated both innovations and acquisitions into an end-to-end customer story, one with a unified user experience and clearly differentiated business model.

Finally, framing at a feature level identified both what to build and how to build it. The product teams used this detailed problem framing to select capabilities to drive individual product roadmaps.

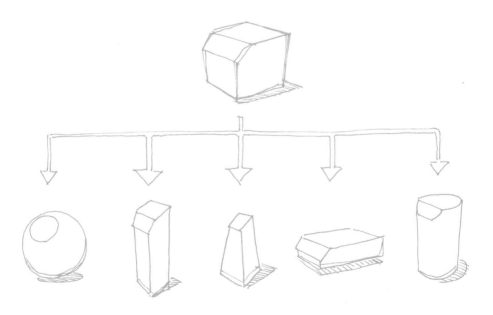

TAKEAWAY

CREATE AND ARTICULATE THE PROBLEM STRATEGY BY TELLING STORIES THAT SHOW AN OPTIMISTIC VISION OF THE FUTURE.

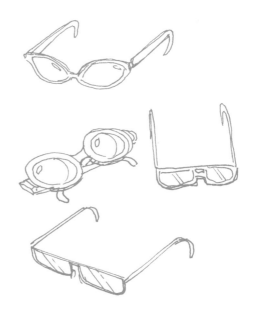

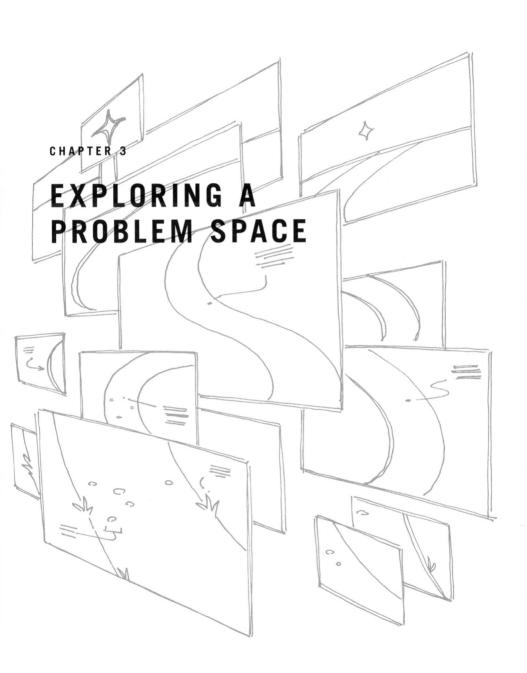

CHAPTER 3

EXPLORING A PROBLEM SPACE

If you lead a creative team, you'll sometimes feel as if your team is not making progress. Everything seems stagnant until, all of a sudden, a proposed solution pops up, seemingly by magic. Where does it *really* come from? It comes from doing the creative work—framing describes the problem, exploration brings up constraints that further define the problem, and constraints inspire the making of artifacts and set the stage for magic to happen.

If you were a fly on the wall in a creative studio, you would probably observe something like this:

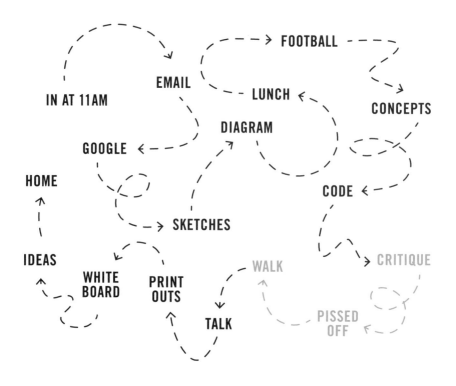

Came in at 11; checked email; looked at Google News. Sketched on the whiteboard; talked through an idea. Scratched out an architectural diagram on the whiteboard. Went to lunch. Tossed a football around the office, while talking some more. Drew some new concepts in Photoshop. Wrote some

code. Had a critique. Got pissed off. Went for a walk. Sat on the couch and talked. Printed some ideas out. Whiteboard. Redid an idea. Again. And Again. Headphones on. Headphones off. Went home.

And at some point, it probably looked like this: *Got hit with a sprint of enthusiasm; 13 hours of sketching. Forgot to eat. Worked until 3am.*

And it almost always includes something like this: *Cat videos. No motivation. Cat videos. Work from home. Sleep. Cat videos. Drink.*

CAT VIDEOS   WORK FROM HOME   CAT VIDEOS   DRINK

NO MOTIVATION   SLEEP

Some of these are caricatures of creative people or environments: tossing the football around, coming in at 11 in the morning. But ignore those for a second. Think about *Had a critique. Got pissed off. Went for a walk.*

Traditionally, feelings have had no place in business, which has been seen as a serious, rational endeavor. But when you introduce creativity into the workplace, it stops being *just business*. The work becomes personal, tied to identity. We take things personally, and we see ourselves reflected in the thing we've made. Critique—which often focuses on the negative—is fundamental to creativity.

REDID AN IDEA. AGAIN. AND AGAIN.

Of course you would save time if you could just get the idea right the first time, but that's not how creativity works. The process of iteration is the only way an idea improves, yet it's time-inefficient, labor-intensive, and often steeped in unintended busywork.

HIT WITH A SPRINT OF ENTHUSIASM; 13 HOURS OF SKETCHING. FORGOT TO EAT. WORKED UNTIL 3AM.

Creativity doesn't happen from 9 to 5. It often happens only when the drive is there, and that drive often manifests as a manic source of production. It's often followed by a depressive rut:

CAT VIDEOS. NO MOTIVATION. CAT VIDEOS. WORK FROM HOME. SLEEP. CAT VIDEOS. DRINK.

The creative process is frustrating to watch. Often the outcome looks so simple that it's hard to justify the weeks and weeks it took to get there. When you look at it and use it, your reaction is often something like, "Of course you would build that; it would be silly not to." The Under Armour shift seems inevitable given the various acquisitions, the proliferation of wearables, and the desire to help customers better understand their bodies. The Bb Planner product seems obvious given the problems facing education. But these solutions are only *obvious in retrospect*—after the team has gone through its strategic, conceptual, and tactical work.

Innovation is like shooting at a moving target. The reason it takes so long to crystalize a new creative idea might not be poor processes or dysfunction. The reason might actually live in the essential process of ideation, which is about making something to gain clarity, not to ship a product. *Making something changes the problem space.* It deepens our knowledge, which we use to make more things, and that makes the idea better and more refined.

This ideation process includes two main forms of movement:

- *iteration*—doing another version of what you just did. Contrary to the adage "insanity is doing the same thing over and over and hoping for different results," iteration calls for *forcing* different results from the same actions. Iteration is about improving quality.

- *variation*—trying many, many different solutions to a single problem. Variation is about quantity, rather than quality.

Both iteration and variation require a unique form of creative management. To understand that form in context, let's return to the concept—and the *point*—of framing: The requirements for creativity emerge from the problem itself, which starts with poorly defined edges. Often, it's not even clear that a problem exists until the ideation process defines it. The team builds tacit knowledge of the problem space by making something. As the team gains clarity, the individual steps towards a solution become more and more accurately defined. The first *making something* may be a sketch on a whiteboard or a napkin. But once it exists, it can go through the iteration process.

Iteration also means bringing improvement, both to the idea and to the fidelity of the idea, with every step. By iterating the thing you made, you take the idea from ambiguity to clarity, which makes it easier and easier to have an opinion about it.

But when people have *varying* opinions, things start to get muddled. Which is the best direction to head? How do we know which idea to pick? Putting the idea through the *variation* process helps to navigate the muddle. This is the process of exploring a solution space by moving sideways beyond the obvious solution to something unexpected and new. It produces a quantity of ideas at each variation and at the same level of fidelity.

The iteration process we've described underscores a simple idea: "One and done" just doesn't work. The iterative style of the creative process has implications on time to market, budget, and the patience necessary to watch bad ideas slowly transform into good ones. Iteration and variation can derail an anticipated budget, the established timeline, a sense of alignment, and even team morale. In this section, I'll describe how to manage creative work and add structure to the ambiguity early in the process.

GETTING IT RIGHT ON THE FIRST TRY

There's a weird expectation in school, business, politics, and even daily life—the idea that we are committed on our first try, that we won't want to undo our actions to try again. It feels as though decisions have permanent implications. Politicians are often derided for "flip-flopping", or changing their mind after publicly committing to a direction, as if a commitment can't be undone.

But most things *can* be undone or, more important, *re*done. If I break something, I can fix it. If I offend someone, I can apologize. And if I make something, I can change it: I can make it again or make more of it or make it better.

In business, we often ignore our flexibility with the things we make. We ignore it for a few reasons. One reason is that the thing we made was so hard to make in the first place that to make it again feels like a huge task. I've seen designers spend weeks and weeks building something before they suddenly realize they've gone astray. It took seeing the design to clarify that and how they could improve it. At that stage, they often give up in frustration. The result seems permanent because changing it feels insurmountable.

Related to the feeling that change is hard is the feeling that change is destructive: "What I have now is the best it's going to get. If I change what I've made, I'll screw it up."

Both of these limitations are driven by a personal block. In the first case, I feel defeated because I feel like I've wasted my time. In the second case, I feel as though I'm not good enough, and I'm somehow unworthy of the result I arrived at.

I remember feeling both of these vividly in design school, particularly in drawing class where we would sketch hundreds of iterations. For me, drawing was really, really hard. What I made didn't look at all like what I wanted, and worse, it didn't look like what the rest of the class was drawing. So on the rare occasion that I made something I was proud of, I was inclined to treat it like a precious object because it would never happen again.

It's a subtle distinction, but I was more concerned with the quality of the execution than the quality of the content. I judged how the thing looked, rather than what it was, and when I had something that looked good enough to keep, I kept it. The surface (my ability to draw) was more important than the content (what I was actually drawing). I kept the wrong things, and I didn't want to draw anymore.

Iteration, on the other hand, encourages us to make informed changes to an existing design. Testing, critique, or simply the act of iterating might inform or provoke these changes. This create-reflect-change process, which can drive some project managers crazy, can look like an endless pursuit of perfection. But it isn't. When I design software or services, for example, I gain a "sweeping sense" of design ideas, but I can't keep all of its details in my head at once. Iteration allows me to infuse this sense into the work and overcome the limitations of my own memory. I first make a "broad stroke," often a diagram, intended to get the essence of the idea out. For a service, this broad stroke typically includes a view of the touch points, the people involved, the handoffs, and a few key details.

Once I've created (drawn, wireframed, coded, modeled, etc.) this broad stroke, its iterations assume the basic framework as fact, as a rigid constraint. Now, I can tell stories about that first state, using scenarios (sometimes called *hero flows)* to expand on how people will experience whatever it is I've made. These stories act as early iterations. I'll refine details and extremities, and I'll review and change aspects of the idea, but the idea itself has come to life.

Serving as creative anchors, these early iterations are steps in the right direction. Each further iteration serves to solidify details and become taken for granted: It becomes fact. And, again, as it does, it becomes problematic because I now have a sense of ownership over it; I'll be reluctant to let it go even when a better idea presents itself.

Let's explore how the iterative creative process works and how to keep ideas flexible in more detail.

STARTING WITH A DIAGRAM

A simple diagram can define a problem and set the stage for innovation, as it did in the following example. A few years ago, when I hadn't yet joined the startup MyEdu, I was in its conference room talking with the main product leader, Frank Lyman, about the startup's goals. He got up and drew three circles on the whiteboard.

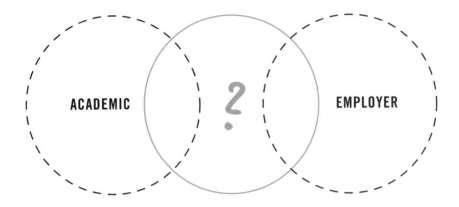

Lyman labeled the first circle *Academic*. He described the startup's already-developed free tools that help students with college. We talked through these tools that hundreds of thousands of students were using each day. Although the tools were massively successful, being free, they weren't generating any revenue for the company.

The second circle was labeled *Employer*. It represented the startup's tools for recruiters, who could sift through students to find attractive job candidates. That was to be the business model of the company—to help students get jobs.

In the middle of the third circle, which connected the other two, Lyman wrote a big question mark. He explained that the startup lacked a way to help students persuade an employer to hire them, and that was the next step in the evolution of the company.

Over time, the question got an answer, something we called a "rich profile"—a tool like LinkedIn but designed specifically for college students. They didn't need to build their profile because the system would do it for them. The more they used our free academic tools, the richer their profile would become, and the more enticing the student would appear to recruiters. Ultimately, the development of this tool was the innovation that led directly to our acquisition. But at the time, it was just a sketch of an incomplete story, poorly drawn, on a whiteboard. It was what you might call a "stupid-simple" sketch.

Lyman later taught me a basic principle that I remember and teach my students. He calls it "simplicity on the other side of complexity." Here's how he explains it.

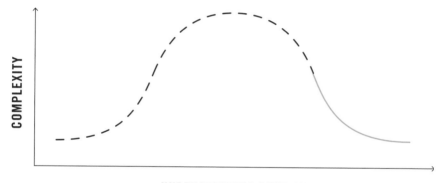

UNDERSTANDING OVER TIME

Draw a basic bell curve. From left to right is understanding, and up and down is complexity. At the left of the diagram, the beginning of taking on a complex problem, you are blissfully naïve. Your descriptions are overly simplistic and reductive. They are based on assumptions stacked on top of guesses, so they are likely wrong and incomplete. Because you don't know what you don't know, your arguments sound poorly thought out, and hard to believe.

As you start to experience more and more, gaining knowledge and insight, you move toward the right of the diagram. You see things from different perspectives, and you start to form an integrative picture of the problem space. At the midpoint—the peak—of the curve, you're seeing the meaning in the data and forming an opinion about it. This means that, to some extent, you *own* the information—it's meaningful to you, so you can act on it.

You can't necessarily *communicate* that information, though. You've integrated it for *yourself*, but that doesn't mean you've distilled it to a meaningful, concise story for someone who's still at the left of the curve. But it's at the midpoint in the curve that people typically *try* to explain complex ideas. Because *they* have all of the data, they think *other people* need all of the data, so they distribute a massive document or spreadsheet or orate an endless meeting. They describe everything they know, and everything they know is overwhelming. The audience often leaves more confused than they started.

Avoid inflicting information overload by continuing to experience things, find that meaning in the data, and revise and recast your opinion. As you do, you'll move beyond the midpoint toward the far right on the curve where informed simplicity lives. It's where you'll be able to not only synthesize the content into your worldview, but also discern the idea's essence in a way that you can communicate to other people. And you'll be able to communicate it so simply and directly that you can also move people with little or no knowledge of the content to the right of the curve.

The place you land on the right—the simplicity on the other side of complexity—is often obvious in retrospect. That's sort of the point: You've made it obvious to others because you did the heavy lifting of getting through the mess.

Lyman borrowed the idea from Oliver Wendell Holmes, the Supreme Court justice who said, "For the simplicity that lies this side of complexity, I would not give a fig, but for the simplicity that lies on the other side of complexity, I would give my life." Lyman's three-circle diagram was simplicity on the other side of complexity. He had been living with an academic suite of products for close to a year, making no money but accumulating tons of users. He had no business model around those products, but over time—through trial, error, conversation, and meaningful reflection, Lyman had worked his way towards a simple framework that represented the direction of the entire company.

When, later, I found myself noodling on the diagram, I realized that in its simplicity was power. Lyman had transferred complex ideas to me in such a simple container. As I drew the diagram, I gained ownership over the knowledge and the problem itself. I realized I actually had a pretty good understanding of the business goal, and I could start to imagine the product suite that would get there.

More important, I saw the opportunity that Lyman saw. His diagram provoked meaning for me because its simplicity was a placeholder for a large, important, and well-considered vision. Lyman hadn't *solved* the problem; he had *synthesized* it into a strong, simple, powerful frame.

TELLING AN END-TO-END STORY

Perhaps one of the most fundamental ways to communicate an idea is through stories. Because they have been part of our lives since we were children, we all know how to listen to them. We know when a story is compelling and feels real, and we know when it feels fake or forced. What's more, we know that when a story is exciting, we want to retell it; it becomes part of us, and we want to share that part with other people.

Creative stories are no different. The first iteration of a creative idea is a story of an optimistic future, one that doesn't yet exist. This story stitches together a new idea with familiar norms, morals, expectations, work patterns, and idiosyncrasies of real people.

This is a way of humanizing new ideas. When we hear about a new product or service, it's common for us to try to fit that new idea into our old worldview. What will this new product feel like? How will I use it? Where will I encounter it? We view the new through a filter of the old, and if the story doesn't mesh, we reject the new idea as being crazy, or far-fetched, or simply not for me.

No matter what the topic, a few elements can make a story come to life.

First, a good story needs believable people. It's *unbelievable* that a grade-school teacher would want to troubleshoot a printer driver, or that a parent would want to refinance a mortgage using a mobile phone, or that a regular rider of a public bus would suddenly buy a Ferrari online. To craft a narrative that's *believable*, we need to start with characters that feel real.

The best way to arrive at a believable character is to spend time with the people you are crafting a picture of. Go watch that grade-school teacher, parent, and bus rider and get to know them. Soon you'll be able to tell a story of their wants and needs, and when you start to drop new, creative ideas in their laps, you'll form a credible product definition.

Next, include goals that are realistic. While the existence of one or two grade-school teachers who want to put their curriculum online is certainly plausible, it's not (yet) realistic to expect that to be a common goal. Instead you need goals that are shared by a bulk of the population. You'll find them through the same observational research you used to find credible people, and both will help you craft a compelling first narrative.

Then paint a picture of how your realistic person will try to reach that realistic goal. Using your new creative idea, articulate the steps, and paint a picture (through both words and images) of that new reality. What does the world look like with this new product and service that helps people do great new things? This is the story to tell—describing a new capability in a regular day in a daily life, as if that capability already existed.

Let's review, to link this idea to the work we've already done. Having articulated a value proposition and north star, we developed specific value-promise statements:

We are designing a tool to help students apply to the right college with the right financial-aid package. **We are designing this for** students, so they can better succeed in their academic journey, but also for parents—to help them make more informed decisions—and for guidance counselors, so they can better manage their limited time and resources. **We promise to**:

› Help students build financial-aid packages with ease, find a school where they will be successful, and apply to that school.

› Help parents better understand the college admissions process, better prepare for the financial burden of college, and support their student in the logistics of a college application (on time, correctly filled out, etc.).

› Help guidance counselors identify the status of each student's application, spread their knowledge to a larger audience, and personally help students who need help the most.

Now, we can start to craft end-to-end stories about how this will happen. We'll develop three hero flows: stories that define an optimistic future in which our product exists, and works perfectly. Each story will substantiate our value promises.

1. Help students build financial-aid packages with ease, find a school where they will be successful, and apply to that school.

Jim is a junior in high school. He has recently started thinking about college, and he has been working with his guidance counselor to develop a strategy for applying to school. She shows him Succeed!, and together they create an account and a profile. Jim uses the tool to describe his family's financial situation and easily puts together a view of his desired financial-aid package. He learns about how interest works, and how it's deferred until he graduates. He also begins to understand how a small loan can compound into something larger.

Based on his interests and passions, Jim identifies several schools in the area. He views videos on their sports programs, dorm life, and his primary interest, marine biology. He can save individual schools to his favorites list.

A few weeks later, Jim has narrowed his list to four schools that are affordable and close to home, and that match his interests. He shares them with his parents, who receive an email link to browse the schools. With a simple click of a button, Jim can leverage the common application to apply to all four schools at once.

2. Help parents better understand the college admissions process, better prepare for the financial burden of college, and support their student in the logistics of a college application (on time, correctly filled out, etc.).

As Jim explores schools, his parents use Succeed! to better understand the school-application process. They create parent accounts, and by linking their account to Jim's, they can see how his search and application are proceeding.

Jim's mom watches several videos about how the application process works. She learns about financial aid, and using a simple calculator, identifies a budget for Jim's education.

Both parents check the career histories of some alumni and find a lot of well-paying jobs in marine biology.

As Jim proceeds through the process, he doesn't understand several questions about his parents' financial history, so he flags the questions where his parents can find them in their own account and fill in that information.

3. Help guidance counselors identify the status of each students' application, spread their knowledge to a larger audience, and personally help students who need help the most.

Nancy, Jim's guidance counselor, is responsible for 150 juniors and seniors who are applying for college. She's always been understaffed and a little overwhelmed, but with Succeed!, she can focus only on the students who need help.

On the tool's application dashboard, Nancy can see a goal and progress bar for each student, identifying their education aspirations and their progress towards completing their application. When she sorts by progress, she spots ten students who haven't yet started the application process so she asks them to schedule a meeting with her.

The tool also helps Nancy easily find students who have set their sights on schools that are unlikely to accept them because their grades are too low. She identifies substitute schools that have similar educational offerings but lower acceptance criteria, and sends these recommendations to students.

Finally, she sees that Jim has submitted his application and his parents have signed off. She sends Jim a message that he'll see next time he logs into Succeed!: "Great job—good luck—can't wait to see what happens next!"

These stories expand on the value proposition and value promises by beginning to gesture to what the product actually does. Generating these stories is a creative act that requires dreaming, but contextualizing those dreams in a sense of reality. The stories are believable because they build on familiar technological and behavioral patterns. It would be unbelievable for Jim to apply to school and get an immediate acceptance or rejection letter. It also would be unbelievable for the tool to automatically scan Jim's parents' credit history and instantly provide a loan. These features would be great, but they rely on infrastructure, policies, or technology that just aren't mature yet.

FORCING A LATERAL PROVOCATION

Creative people will often describe *playing with an idea*. What do they mean? How can you play with something that isn't tangible?

Ideas can feel alive, and they change and morph through the creative process. Play is one of the best ways to help an idea evolve; wordplay—manipulating the actual language of an idea—is one of the most fundamental ways to explore. Let's take a look at how that works.

> Back at Succeed!, you're working on a tool intended to help students succeed in college by taking the right classes at the right time.
>
> You might start with a traditional, conservative articulation of the product's value: Plan your schedule. Schedule-planning is a utility that you would typically build and move on. But first, let yourself free-associate off the word "schedule," and see where you end up.
>
> For example, the word might make you think of time, and "time" could lead you to the "sands of time"—the hourglass, with a trickle of sand falling from one bulb to the other. Sand, in turn, might prompt ideas about the ocean and the beach. The free association is a chain, moving quickly from one idea to the other.
>
> So, we have "Schedule", "Sand", "Hourglass", "Ocean" and "Beach." What can we do with that?

What if managing a schedule were more like looking at the vast expanse of potential classes (a beach) and building a schedule out of the sand? And why not? During the planning process, schedules can be flexible: you can build a schedule, explore its trajectory, take pride in what you've made, and knock it down, as if it were a sand castle.

This style of wordplay led MyEdu to a planning tool that does those things: It allows a student to build a schedule, look at it, knock parts of it down, and rebuild them in a new way. The planner leveraged a design principle of impermanence, so students could change their mind. They took full advantage of that principle. The schedule-planning tool was one of MyEdu's most used products (and before MyEdu's 2012 acquisition, the company boasted more than 2 million users).

Take a second and reflect on how you felt as you read this story of wordplay. Chances are, you felt one of two things. You might have felt that it made a lot of sense: Each word built on the last, creating a landscape of metaphor that drove a new way of thinking about—and a new solution to—an old problem.

Or, you might have discounted the entire process out of hand. You might have thought, "That's obvious—of course you would want to try on schedules rather than just locking in to one." But thinking that the end is obvious, although common, is fair only in retrospect. When such thinkers see the end, they get the benefit of a backwards trail: There's an inevitability to it.

This wordplay is a part of a broader creative strategy called lateral thinking—a creative process of thinking "around" an idea. That improves on the typical linear way of attempting to solve a problem.

Here's an example of linear thinking:

At Succeed!, we're trying to solve a problem related to students dropping out of school. First, we might try to identify why they drop out. Academia is expensive; it seems to make sense that the cause is high tuition costs, and research supports that idea. So we would walk a linear path from that cause to a solution. We can help students deal with high tuition by giving them loans. We can provide loans based on students' ability to repay those loans. We can look at their credit and employment histories to approve students for a loan.

We've identified a path that tracks in a thoughtful way from problem to solution. This form of linear thinking is safe because each assumption along the way seems reasonable. It makes sense to think students drop out because they can't pay, that a loan is a reasonable response to inability to pay, and that loans should be secured based on credit history.

But that sensible, reasonable path doesn't allow for the breadth of innovative thinking. Imagine tracking the path of a seemingly unrelated provocation towards a solution. In that case, "logical" and "linear" aren't much help.

Try this out, and see how you feel about the process.

Why do students drop out? Because they don't have any beautiful flowers.

Wait, what? What do flowers have to do with academic attrition?

Explore a chain of words related to flowers: the word itself, then beauty, color, happiness, sunshine, warmth, growth, hugs. The words spark other, related terms; it's a chain of ideas, and we can follow that chain forever. Because the words have no clear link to academia, we *could* dismiss them out of hand. Instead, let's give them a chance.

Warmth, growth, hugs—without hugs, perhaps people feel alone, and when they do, perhaps they drop out. What if we could give students virtual *hugs,* at the moment when they feel down? What if we could surprise them with *flowers* in their dorm room during final exams? What if students could share incomplete projects with other classmates, who could build on those ideas—prompting *growth?*

| FLOWERS | BEAUTY | COLOR | HAPPINESS | SUNSHINE | WARMTH | GROWTH | HUGS |

Let's try the exercise with another provocation based on why students might be dropping out. This time, let's go with something really arbitrary: *combination locks.*

| LOCK | SECURITY | CONTROL | SECRET | STEEL | HARDENED | RIGID | CLOSED |

Again, the prompt sparks relationships—lock, security, control, secret, steel, hardened, rigid, closed. Also as before, while the relationships don't clearly link to education, we can find our way around to the topic if we try: Students aren't in *control*. The academic process feels *closed* and *rigid*. Students can't find the *secret* to success because they feel as though it's *locked* away from them. The lateral connection opens up new ways to think about old problems.

Our prompts—*students drop out because they don't have any flowers* and *students drop out because of combination locks*—assert a deliberately absurd, unreasonable form of causality. But although they don't mirror our understanding of the world, as provocations, these phrases are hugely valuable.

Unlike established connections, like high tuition as a cause of attrition, these lateral connections seem obvious only in retrospect. The spreading word-to-word activation leads to unexpected paths. Those unexpected paths activate new solution spaces in the brain, which in turn lead to unexpected problem frames. By pursuing a path of lateral thinking, problem frames can emerge in innovative ways. Simply, lateral thinking forces creativity.

The ideas that lateral thinking generates are fragile, though. It's too easy to write them off. Rigid, logical business cultures often view this type of thinking as childish, irrational, unproductive, and maybe even "dumb." They implicitly sweep it aside, while supporting proposals, agendas, and ideas backed by hard data. In a culture that supports and funds only linear ideas, lateral thinking can't win.

Instead, this innovative approach to innovation requires a culture that embraces this sort of play. Employees in this culture feel encouraged to try on these new ideas and see where they go.

My lateral-thinking workshops with executives produce a variety of reactions. People from creative cultures tend to wordplay with abandon. Because they don't worry about how others will perceive their ideas, they tend to generate more ideas, and less predictable or logical ones. On the other hand, executives from other types of cultures often ask whether they are "doing it right". They tend to look for a single correct answer and avoid risky ideas. And they often discount the entire process as silly, juvenile, or a waste of time.

Rules are based on logical responses to potential situations; the presence of a lot of corporate policies and rules usually is a sign that lateral thinking won't survive. If a company penalizes employees for not submitting a timely expense report, for not following some other documented procedure, or for putting pictures on the wall, employees quickly learn to standardize on logical responses to prompts rather than unexpected ones. The rules seem to say, "we value rule-following more than rule-breaking." Lateral thinking breaks the rules with language.

Humor is deeply linked to lateral thinking (in fact, a joke's punch line, which is often nonsensical ahead of time but obvious in retrospect, can be a form of lateral thinking); a culture that supports humor typically supports these lateral leaps. Often, off-color humor is actually an indicator of this type of culture. This isn't to say we should all be telling offensive jokes, but consider how a lack of political correctness could be tied to a permissive culture. If I worry that someone will audit my jokes for appropriateness, I probably worry about that someone auditing my *ideas*.

Another signal of lateral thinking can be *free-form* brainstorming. This brainstorming method has nothing to do with those boring meetings where people talk in circles or in group-think (narrowing to one idea rather than inviting an assortment). In cultures that encourage free-form brainstorming, lateral thinking flourishes.

To recap, here are the signs of a creative culture that embraces lateral thinking:

- Open to non-obvious, often irrational ideas. Ideas that seem not to make sense receive runway for exploration. People consider themselves "free enough" that they can explore ideas like these, even if the ideas go nowhere.

- Supporting word play. They link ideas to words and embrace word relationships.

- Lacking rules and policies. Lateral thinking breaks established norms, and a culture that allows actual rule breaking also allows idea-based rule breaking.

- Focusing on quantity of new ideas, rather than on fidelity of one idea.

It's hard to shift a culture, particularly one infused with staid thinking. It's not good enough to simply bring in people who are open to irrational ideas or who tend to reject policy and rules out of hand—they will be like salmon, swimming against the current. Instead, a cultural shift around these ideas takes time and needs to be (somewhat ironically) logically and methodically designed. This strategic shift is as important as identifying new markets or launching new products and services.

To make that shift, as a leader, you can compensate, promote, and reward people who play and explore. Make it obvious that playful and eccentric employees are promoted. And you can analyze and remove pointless rules and policies that have "always been there."

REMOVE RULES, REWARD PLAY, AND MAKE IT CLEAR THAT YOU VALUE EXPLORATION OVER RESULTS.

LEVERAGE ANALOGOUS SITUATIONS

You may have identified an initial topic area, conducted research, and even synthesized the research into meaningful insights. The emotionally harder part can be identifying what to build. What will be your preliminary set of features or capabilities? I've seen technologists who must rework code because they fear building the wrong thing, product managers who aren't yet confident in their product decisions, and designers who stall on synthesizing research—all of these situations can culminate in a culture of inaction. In many ways, methods like "Lean" and "Agile" are a way of getting over this hump; they encourage trying to build something super-small and super-fast, and to "fail early and often." Other ways to identify a resonant set of features can be less troublesome and more effective. These include identifying an analogous emotional experience and mapping the interactions over time.

By identifying an analogous emotional experience, you can understand and leverage emotional inflection points.

First, think about the insights and goals you've identified through your research. If you are working in the space of medicine, you might have described insights like, "People want to stay healthy with minimal effort" or "People don't understand or trust scientific terms for medical conditions." You might have identified goals like, "Safely treat a disease" or "Understand treatment plans."

Now, based on the goals and insights, describe the uniquely human interactions and emotions that are typical when people try to achieve their goals. Interactions and emotions related to safely treating a disease might include, "Remember to take a pill each day," "Feel confident of progress being made," and "Check in with a professional once a month." Those related to understanding treatment plans might include, "Read about the treatment plan in plain language," "Discuss complexities with other people," and "Feel in control."

Now, think about a comparable—an "analogous"—situation that has nothing to do with health care. In what are other situations are all of these qualities true?

- Remember to do something each day.

- Feel confident of progress being made.

- Check in with a professional once a month.

- Read about the situation in plain language.

- Discuss complexities with other people.

- Feel in control.

You can find an analog in things like gardening, working toward an executive MBA, and training for a marathon. All of these endeavors require daily interactions, have a long and slow sense of progress, require infrequent but regular professional interactions, have lots of jargon that can be described in plain language, might involve discussions of complexities with other people, and require a feeling of control.

For example, take training for a marathon, and begin to describe how the process happens over time. Sketch a timeline and describe the main artifacts to support people as they train. For example, people wear *devices* to track their progress through the day, and coaches prepare *calendars* to remind runners of their training regimen; people join *groups* to receive encouragement and help, and people read *magazines* with inspirational stories of people just like them, succeeding.

All of these artifacts become prompts for your brand new product in health care, offering initial touch points, and pointing at potential features for your new product. Ponder the calendar idea, the group idea, the magazines, and the devices, and think about why these are so effective in the analogous situation. Then, freely steal the ideas, and apply them to the new context.

This method of looking at analogous situations requires a rich enough view of the world to even think of marathon training or gardening. In addition to this technique as a prompt for momentum, consider how you can more generally broaden your view of culture and society. Ideas might include reading new blogs that have nothing to do with software or startups, and going to conferences that are two or three times removed from your comfort zone.

PROTOTYPING IDEAS

Making things takes time and energy. It takes blocks of reserved, uninterrupted, and focused thought and effort. Before making things can help to clear up ambiguity, it must exist in the presence of ambiguity. So a creative company empowers *making* at a strategic and conceptual level. Of course that company must also cover the tactical level, by giving employees the room and tools to make things.

The thing we make to represent and explore something new is known as a *prototype*. Rather than just words or a specification that describes an idea, a prototype *shows* the idea and often lets someone experience it. Prototypes take on an increasingly important role in describing the largely invisible and hard-to-describe ideas of a digital future. For example, while a self-driving car looks at least slightly different than a regular one, the innovation shift is almost entirely in software. A prototype of the idea gives form that people can experience, and that experience gives the idea credibility.

With a prototype, you can ground criticism in that reality of experience; the experience, then, connects the idea directly to value. Think a bit about what it means to critique an experience, rather than an idea. Experience is about feeling over time, colored by the connection between emotions in the present and by memories of experiences. Audiences bring their history to an experience, so that experience is personal. The evaluation of an experience can be rich, informed by a visceral emotional sense, and not just an analytical evaluation.

A creative culture embraces prototypes as a means of exploration. It *expects* employees to make prototypes, and it communicates that expectation through example: Leaders develop concepts, prototypes, sketches, and artifacts that represent complex ideas. Demos of interactive simulations take on more value than presentations and documents; the prototype of an idea carries more weight than the idea itself. The company also conveys its prototype expectation through compensation structures that reward makers.

"Demo or die" is the motto of the MIT media lab, considered one of the world's most creative idea labs. Co-Founder Nicholas Negroponte, known for his One Laptop Per Child initiative, describes how demonstrations act as proof of an idea and its value: "Forget technical papers and, to a lesser extent, theories. Let's prove by doing. Many folks in traditional computer science still think that 'demo or die' is all about icing and cake. Wow, are they wrong." (Markoff, 1996)

To demonstrate a product, a service, or an organizational model means taking pride in the artifact's creation. It also means recognizing that an artifact and the idea it represents are never truly complete. A company that embraces early prototypes also embraces a culture of incompleteness that nurtures a fledgling idea instead of destroying it. Imagine the confidence it takes to demonstrate an incomplete idea. Demonstration means trusting the audience to understand and evaluate a prototype. We trust the audience to see through the broken parts and incompleteness to judge the idea on the experience itself.

Tom Chi, a Co-Founder of Google X, describes that he "prototyped a fully working heads-up display on Day 1 of the Google Glass project, constructed from a coat hanger, a piece of Plexiglas that happened to be lying around, a sheet protector bought from the local convenience store, a little wire harness, and a netbook." (Khan, 2012) The audience was able to see beyond the raw materials to the idea itself. A prototype overcomes a "guessathon," he says—*thinking* something will work, rather than *learning* it will. "[People say] 'Oh, I think in three weeks we can do that.' 'I think this will work.' 'I think users will prefer this over that.' These are things you probably hear a thousand times every day, at work. ...Just make the thing, just make it work, and start to learn things."

The cultural shift from talking and guessing to showing, experiencing, and proving can start in a top-down manner. Leadership can start asking and requiring demonstrations, not just presentations. If you cancel or reschedule meetings without demos, the expectation will start to become clear. This shift from a talking culture to a prototyping culture can also come bottom-up. Individual contributors can start to make actual representations of ideas, rather than meta-artifacts that discuss the ideas.

The shift from talking to making forces iterations. It becomes the way ideas roll forward, gaining momentum and clarity. A culture that embraces speed of exploration and proof, like Chi's Google Glass prototype, is one that also embraces iterative, constant improvement. Let's take a look at how an entire market segment emerged through this form of iterative prototyping.

The case of BodyMedia, an innovator in the personal, wearable health-tracking market, is one of constant improvement through prototyping.

(Velazco, 2013). The vision for the wearable tracking products emerged through an iterative process that spanned over a decade of experiences. In the moment, each experience seemed unrelated to another, but in retrospect, these experiences point to the power of iteration over the long haul.

Ivo Stivoric, who, like Chi, works at Google X on the senior leadership team, was the co-founder of BodyMedia and the VP of Research and Development at Jawbone, which acquired BodyMedia. He first began exploring the wearable space as a grad student at Carnegie Mellon University (CMU) in the late 1990s. At CMU's Engineering Design Research Center, Stivoric and his team focused on reducing the time needed to maintain US military vehicles. The researchers identified that workers needed both hands free to do their job in cumbersome physical positions.

The team solved the problem with a hip-mounted circular dial for navigating content on a heads-up display. The research also produced a seed of creative inspiration. Almost as an afterthought, the team wrote, "We were also interested in generality and in furthering our agenda of wearable computers. Thus, we not only focused on the inspection process but also put some thought into the other types of applications for which the device we were constructing could be used." (Bass, et al., 1997)

A year later, the researchers published a seminal paper that identified generalized lessons learned from their military experiences. This paper described 13 guidelines for wearability, including body placement, weight, sensory interaction, and aesthetics. The team concluded that the study "represents a start at putting this information together, organized, in one place, to be useful as a set of guidelines and a resource for designers that need to integrate issues of wearability into a design." (Gemperle, Kasabach, Stivoric, Bauer, & Martin, 1998)

Recall the idea of "obvious in hindsight." As the story of BodyMedia evolves, you'll see key milestones that, in retrospect, look like obvious stepping stones towards success. This paper is one of them.

The team spun this wearable work into an incubator called Sandbox Advanced Development. There the team explored non-military uses for the research. Astro Teller, Stivoric's partner in grad school and now the CEO of Google X, explains, "There's an amazing opportunity to design a computer that people can carry around on their bodies [and] that knows what they want to do and can help them do it." (Kovatech, 1994)

The vision for a health monitoring system emerged. Stivoric explains that the team essentially camped out in a war room and explored a more global story of humanizing computing. "We had a larger vision: How is computing going to change if we never know anything about the individual? If you stopped a person on the street and said, 'Hey, I do wearable computers,' they were scratching their head." In the late 90s, there was no obvious "humanized" application of wearables. The team looked at its wearable research and started canvasing what Stivoric calls "whitespace."

Often, research and development efforts start with a given technology and look for ways to transfer and leverage it into consumer products. This method is, "technology looking for a problem." But instead of a technology vision, Stivoric's team rallied around a guiding user-centered vision. The focus was on making wearable computing more familiar, rather than finding a way to apply a technological advancement—the wearable design developed for the military.

In the search for contexts for wearability, the team spent time with triathletes, cardiologists, and people dealing with weight management. At the same time, the team canvassed emergent technology in early cellphones and sensors. Slowly, a story emerged around a wearable health monitor and a business to support tracking health and wellness. In 2000, the team again reorganized, this time as BodyMedia.

Stivoric explains, "we didn't know where the business was really going to go in terms of where we were going to find our first opportunities." The vision emerged through years of research and through "vectors" of exploration coming together. BodyMedia was the synthesis of a vector on wearable computing, a vector on health care, a vector on the shrinking costs of mobile technology, and a large guiding principle of humanizing technology. That synthesis "became a believable story for people—that the world has to move this way."

Over the next ten years, that guiding principle helped focus the product efforts. The vision didn't focus the company's efforts on just a single product innovation—it acted as a motivator for the team as a viable business slowly emerged. "If you look at our business plan in the early days, we thought we were going to have a full product line of 20 SKUs and we would be in retail stores within five years. The market just wasn't ready for it..."

The company tried different contexts, generating data from a variety of tests and showing them to potential partners like Jenny Craig and Kaiser. The process was tedious. "We talked to doctors, and they would say, 'Well, I get paid $10,000 a surgery, so why are you going to give me a vest or some wearable? I want to cut somebody open [and} stick this thing in here, and I get a $10,000 check; that's the best thing for me and the patient."

The company met similar resistance in the professional-athlete category and the health-care-insurance market, Stivoric says, "Every time we spin up the project team [to explore another topic], we have somebody holding the torch in what both the strategy and vision are along the way." Each iteration narrowed and focused the creative output, but the vision never fundamentally changed.

One of the prime ways to remind people of that vision is with real data. Stivoric recommends that innovators do the following: "Show what data we're getting from people. Show them why there's a reason to believe." Those data have to come from real trials and from pursuit of simultaneous bets. For him, a key to the success of a creative project is identifying the "kill criteria" up front. These are the quantifiable reasons to end a project. Key project requirements come with "an asterisk that says, 'if you can't manage this requirement, we're going to kill the project.' We try to do that in advance."

After burning through three rounds of capital over four years, BodyMedia's primary offering started to solidify. (Wysocki, 2001) By 2005, the company had sold more than 7500 armbands in a market that included offerings from Timex, Nike, and Polar. (Crissey, 2005) That market began to show convergence of data tracking—tracking exercise, nutritional intake, and the "millions of data points" that Teller describes are "spewed" off your body per second. (Murphy, 2005) By the time the company was acquired, it had more than 700,000 users—many on a subscription basis—and was selling devices at a $200 price point. (Dolan, 2011)

From Stivoric's experience with BodyMedia, we can see several primary fundamentals emerge:

First, the product that seems obvious in retrospect came through years of prototypes. The iterations often seemed only tangentially related to one another; research into military maintenance led to research on wearables, which led to research in health care, and so on. It's only now with the benefit of hindsight that we can string continuity between these iterations.

Next, a shared high-level vision of humanizing technology, which oper-ates outside of a particular application of technology, led the team. Before the success of BodyMedia, the team's innovation was in the relationship between technology and people—not in any given algorithm or software IP.

As the team iterated and explored "whitespace" opportunities, it had both implicit and explicit "kill criteria" to help identify and short-circuit ineffective exploration. This shows that leadership needs the confidence to kill a product without simultaneously killing the team's momentum; leadership needs to maintain fidelity around the company's vision, independent of any one product's manifestation of that vision.

Finally, real data provided motivation, proved momentum, and grounded the high-level vision in reality. They also enriched prototypes' fidelity, which meant that the team could actually use them.

Stivoric has brought the same philosophy to Google X, where his teams actively *try* to kill projects. He explains that his team "checks their ego at the door and tries to kill the project early so that we don't spend five years and hundreds of millions of dollars" to find out that the project won't succeed. The team pushes multiple bets at once, and emphasizes shipping products early so that they can benefit from and leverage real data in support of a larger vision.

For the BodyMedia team, prototyping occurred in a progressively narrow span of influence. The first iterations were, strategically speaking, at a "50,000 foot view"—including even what industry segment to play in. Over almost 15 years, the iterations became narrower and narrower, and when the company was acquired, in 2016, it was iterating at the product-detail level. It launched the LINK Weight Management System, the LINK Body Monitoring Armband, the bodybuggSP personal calorie management system, the GoWear fit Lifestyle, and other devices—each an iteration in its own right.

We can see from the BodyMedia story that the creative process is one of ideation combined with explicit critique (often driven by the market and usage data itself)—and that each iteration extracts constraints that act as criteria for the next round of iterations.

Stivoric's experiences with iterations match Tom Chi's experiences with creating rough prototypes for Google Glass. They reflect the ethos at Google X around iteration and prototyping. That ethos flourishes in a company culture that recognizes early-stage ideas as poorly formed explorations, not presentations. Such a culture demands, and rewards, constant iteration and evolution, rather than a sense of finality and completeness.

ITERATE THROUGH PROTOTYPING RATHER THAN TALKING. CREATE A CULTURE OF MAKING BY ASKING TO SEE INCOMPLETE IDEAS, RATHER THAN POLISHED ONES.

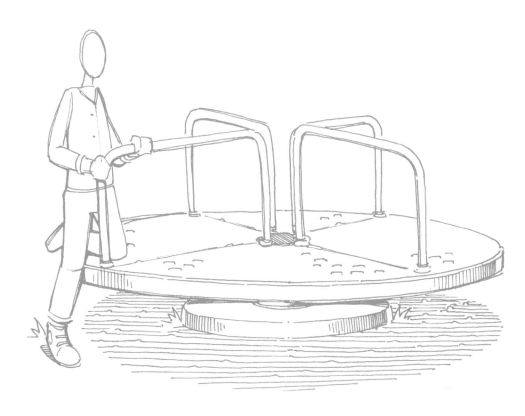

CHAPTER 4

MANAGING SPIN

Creativity is often hampered by *spin*: wasted creative cycles that stall ideas. Despite the techniques you've already learned—storytelling, diagramming, lateral provocations, and thinking about analogous situations—problems can still seem intractable. When spin occurs, designers start to second- and third-guess their decisions and are unable to achieve a harmonious creative state. The creative quality will suffer, as will timelines and budgets. To overcome the negative state of spin, we need to revisit where ideas come from.

THE SEEDS OF A CREATIVE IDEA

In creative professions, so much rests on the *thing being made* because it carries a sense of the creator in it. This is one of the reasons that the "shipping product" can be so important to product teams: When the product ships (launches), they get to see real people using the thing they made, and they can take pride in having produced something of value to the world. Consider those facts in juxtaposition to the culture of meetings, conversation, and discussion that underscore a lot of traditional business careers. These traditional business structures often ignore real people, both the users and the makers.

Judy Siegel is the Director of User Experience at MSNBC Digital. Her teams' work often touches politically charged topics, like the 2016 election. Desires to make something that has impact and affects social change are what drives her teams. That means that they want their artifacts to have as large an audience as possible.

Because creative teams care so much about their work, Siegel says, the work can be emotional: "Creativity in business might feel more like therapy… For journalists, I think writing…is therapeutic. To write something, putting the research, time, and energy—and have it published, and be able to look at it and think 'I created something that now lives in the world and hopefully has some value to someone. I did that myself.'"

At MSNBC, Siegel says, creative teams "… want to feel like they're contributing something beautiful to the world. They're contributing something that has value. Maybe it has a message that will change someone's mind [or] something that creates a memory that somebody will keep." Prematurely cutting a project undermines that feeling of contribution.

The output is as important to its maker as the process is, so teams expect their artifacts to actually launch, or be published or produced. Employee retention links to happiness, and happiness links to artifacts being useful. But executives, ignoring the project team, often kill incomplete projects because of budgets or company reorgs. Employee attrition grows with the frequency of those "murders": They have tremendous emotional impact on a team that derives personal satisfaction and measures personal and professional growth on artifacts finding their way into the world.

Burnout, linked to killed projects, is an unfortunate part of the creative process, too. I've seen some of my best employees come into work, turn on their computers, stare blankly, and accomplish nothing. It's not laziness. This component of spin is a feeling of hopelessness that creates inertia. And it festers—the entire creative team can get pulled into one person's rut and take the whole project down with them.

To counter the inertia, we need a creative momentum builder.

Momentum or creative energy comes from a variety of places but rarely, in contrast to popular belief, in a "eureka" moment of insight. Instead, according to most creativity research, it comes through a more methodical and often-implicit process that stretches over time. This process typically contains several key ingredients.

1. **Recombining existing ideas in new ways triggers new ideas.** For example, what happens when you combine the idea of sharing with home ownership? What happens when you combine robotics with vehicles?

   These creative ideas lie bubbling below the surface, waiting for some form of creative clarity. That clarity emerges as combinations come together, sometimes forced, sometimes organically. It also emerges over time, which means you can't rush creativity. Give it a runway and time for stewing over ideas.

   As combinations spark ideas, *unexpected* combinations spark unexpected ones. This means that we'll benefit from a diverse input to the creative process, which runs counter to our typical behavior: We tend to immerse ourselves in our expertise. So, for example, if we are in education, we read education blogs, go to education conferences, and study other education products.

But it's creative inspiration from *outside* disciplines that provokes new ways of considering old ideas. A team that's encouraged to explore beyond the context of company's subject-matter expertise will be more successful in establishing novel ideas than a team that stays in its lane.

2. **Creative momentum often comes from informed trial and error.** And it does so at a more tactical level, not just a vision one. Consider how visual designers might go about their work. They move elements around on the screen, trying things, erasing things, positioning and repositioning elements. Their iterations happen in rapid-fire succession. The process of trying things informs the next iteration, and it happens so quickly that it appears not to happen at all.

   Nor do these iterations leave a trail. Their creators aren't saving iterations of every state. They may not even be aware of their "moves." The artifact itself supplies the inspiration for the artifact, where each change is the impetus for the next one. This means that creators' output may not be rational; after the artifact's creation, its creators may find it difficult to explain and justify the artifact.

3. **Outright theft can drive creative momentum.** Good designers borrow, it is said, but great designers steal. Creative people are constantly studying and appropriating the stylistic and content decisions of other creative people. This appropriation result in industry patterns and trends, along with a "sameness" in creative assets.

Supporting creative inspiration means recognizing that each method requires time for exploration. As a creative leader, you must provide it. You must protect the team from meetings, readouts, working sessions, and other forced collaborations. Put control back into the hands of your team members, so they can explore for as long as they need to develop a solution that's both innovative and well crafted.

THE HARMONY OF FLOW

Have you ever worked on a problem with such intensity that you lost track of time? Then something snapped you out of that trance-like work state, and you realized that you hadn't had an introspective thought in some time. It almost appeared as if you weren't there. These, and several other qualities, describe a creative state called flow. According to psychologist Mihaly Csikszentmihalyi, the flow achieved during creativity is "an almost automatic, effortless, yet highly focused state of consciousness." During this state, you can move through the space of a problem, suspending self-criticism and trying multiple ideas without self-censoring.

Flow is about a vivid awareness of the moment but an almost lack of awareness of the surrounding environment and task. During flow, the sense of self and self-consciousness disappears. While experiencing flow, people become too involved in their activities to worry about protecting their self-image or ego. As a result, their work output flourishes—they produce better results.

Let's try it. Take a second, look up, and adjust your mind's eye to view the scene in front of you in the whole. Literally and figuratively "sit back" to experience the scene. Now, focus in on one specific piece of the landscape in front of you. Try to block out everything else from your periphery, drilling as deeply as you can into that one object. Think about it in as much detail as you can; see if you can flip it over in your mind and see it from multiple sides.

When your creative perspective is broad—often when you are well rested and without stress or anxiety—you can literally see more things in your field of vision. You're more likely to feel an active curiosity, look for things to learn about and experience, and be open to new ideas, actively. You can traverse relationships between ideas in a playful way.

Conversely, when you are concerned or anxious about something, or when you are coping with chaos, or solving a problem—you can feel your vision constricting. You might find yourself ignoring your surroundings and focusing on a single, narrow problem. A laptop or whiteboard becomes the sole focus of your attention—it actually becomes an extension of your thoughts. It enhances the tunneling, making it extraordinarily hard to attend to outside influences. You pay no attention to the world around you or outside influences. This is a productive perspective.

Neither perspective is better than the other, but the deep and narrow focus is the one that's deeply related to flow. Expertise and an appropriate amount of challenge are two factors in this narrow perspective. The onus is on you as a creative director to stretch your team's creative limits and prevent boredom.

Next, flow requires a feeling of effortless control. This comes from safety—a feeling that nothing is actually riding on the results, and so the results are ends in themselves. This means finding ways to hide, at least temporarily, deadlines and the relative importance of creative output. Showing your team how critical their work is to the business while giving them space to forget that while they work is a tricky line to walk.

Finally, flow takes blocks of undisturbed time. A culture that recognizes the importance of flow can create a virtual barrier around a creative team. If you empower the team to act autonomously, they can move quickly and produce things faster. Conference calls, meetings, check-ins, standups, email threads, bug-lists, IMs, and other distractions, on the other hand, can make it impossible to enter this flow-like state. Someone who is checking in with the team or waiting for consensus cannot enter this state.

The actual rules of the business prevent entering flow, too. For example, many companies force employees to use locked-down computers, obey various security protocols, and even enforce their ability to organize their own creative space. Some companies even prohibit staff from hanging things on the wall.

These rules are often in place for good reason. The company may need to comply with industry regulations or to actively protect intellectual property. But these policies oppose the seeds of creativity. Company leaders must understand that compliance can have a negative effect on creativity. A company that supports a policy through aggressive restrictions on technological freedom shows that it values IT data protection over creativity.

On the other hand, when a creative team feels free to make independent decisions, creativity flourishes. They experience the joy and flow of intrinsic motivation—the idea that the work is an end in itself. They've embraced the work because it is interesting, personally challenging, and satisfying.

TAKEAWAY

PROTECT YOUR TEAM'S TIME, SO THEY CAN CREATE IN UNINTERRUPTED BLOCKS.

THE INTERCONNECTEDNESS OF CREATIVE WORK

So, flow comes from internal connection with the work, and leadership that provides a clear conducive environment. Part of clearing the lane for that idealized state is managing feedback. Although structured criticism is fundamental to a creative process, unstructured offhand criticism is harmful. Let's examine how it happens and how to prevent it.

When a creative team is excelling, other groups in the organization notice. They want to associate with the energy of creativity, so they interfere. They offer their opinions. The team, after considering the feedback, might respond by saying it'll take weeks to make those changes.

The product managers or other stakeholders who give the feedback rarely understand why the changes take so long. Beyond the need for time to establish flow, the other reasons for the lengthy process lie in the interconnectedness of the creative process and in the nature of artifacts—and of stakeholders. As a design gains fidelity, sketches and other artifacts become more and more realistic and take longer and longer to make.

Business needs change, and so do perspectives. Often, seeing the actual designs at that high level of fidelity helps the team realize that the sketch is not, in fact, what they want. So the leaders decide to change the work. Maybe they ask for seemingly inconsequential changes, which can still take a long time because a single change will flow through many places. For example, for a design for a mobile-phone application, stakeholders might ask to move a navigation component or change the color. The changes trigger a ripple effect on every screen in the artifact: a series of sketches showing how one tap leads to another.

There's no way to completely eliminate this problem because, as we've seen, creativity simply takes time. But a shortcut to this process is formal, upfront critique. Think of feedback as a funnel, opening from left to right; the funnel represents the amount of time a seemingly simple change makes to a design. Early in the process—on the left—you can quickly make even big changes to creative work because the fidelity of the artifacts and the idea itself are so incomplete. As the idea gains fidelity, so too do the artifacts that represent it. As the idea becomes more established, changes take longer and longer to make. To try to minimize time-consuming downstream changes, include leadership early in the ideation process. This is no silver bullet, though, because to really understand the idea, the team needs to see it. Once they see it, they want to change it.

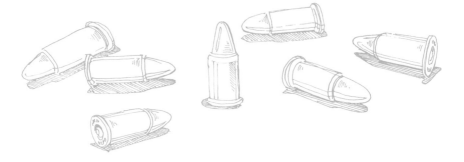

PUSH CREATIVE INVOLVEMENT UPFRONT. RECOGNIZE AND PLAN FOR EXPONENTIAL TIME INCREASES BASED ON FEEDBACK.

THE VALUE OF USER FEEDBACK

One of the keys to creative work is an audience. To ensure user engagement, you don't need a formal and rigorous script or testing protocol. One of the core tenets of both lean product development and design thinking is to "get out of the building." That idea addresses the need to get work in front of a real audience in a casual setting to gauge understanding and reactions. Those reactions indicate whether the work has meaning and fits into someone's life. This attempt to show the appeal of the idea is sometimes called concept testing.

Getting out of the building is also useful for testing the *details* of the work: the parts that the audience criticizes, embraces, notices, and ignores. That feedback informs iterations.

One of the most important parts of showing work to an audience has, ironically, nothing to do with the audience. The acts of preparing, showing, and evaluating work build confidence and affirm the work's goodness. They make a statement, "I made this thing" and validate it. Seeing someone else engage with the idea brings it to life. For a creative team, these user-feedback sessions are milestones, albeit soft and continuous ones. They're emotional guideposts of completion.

Structuring these types of interactions is fairly easy. You don't need to carefully select a "representative sample": users who represent a particular profile or demographic. You also don't need fancy recording equipment or a formal recruiting process. The team simply needs artifacts and the courage to leave the studio.

The research site can be a nearby coffee shop. One or two members of the creative team show the artifacts to the audience, write down the feedback, and bring the work back to the studio to discuss. At this point, you might have to remind the team that what they did in the field was not meant to prove anything. Its value is in provoking iteration and inspiration.

But because the work is not "finished," teams are often reluctant to show it to an audience. They may fear a negative critique or that the work fails to represent the concept well enough. Or sometimes, they fear the actual human-to-human interaction. So your job as a creative leader includes structuring and encouraging regular user engagement in the real world.

You may find that you have to create a strong sense of urgency to get junior staff, in particular, to leave the shelter of the creative office. Act as a guide, helping to prepare the work and maybe literally transporting them to the testing location. Similar to the fear of public speaking, the fear of public *testing* is unfounded, but needing practice to overcome.

The process of user feedback requires rhythm and repetition. The more regular these visits become, the more they will feel like just part of the process. The team will eventually start to proactively seek out user feedback.

LEAVE THE BUILDING TO TALK TO REAL PEOPLE ABOUT REAL WORK.

CHAPTER 5

RUNNING A CRITIQUE

At its most basic level, a critique is a conversation aimed at identifying—*and fixing*—problems. You probably have sat through a conversation that turned into a free-for-all, with everyone piling on some poor team member. A critique can feel like a pile-on because its purpose is to point out things that are wrong. But a *good* critique leaves both parties—those providing critique and those receiving it—in a positive emotional state.

Good critiques are hard because creativity is multi-layered. It's impossible to discuss a creative solution intelligently and constructively without intimate knowledge of that solution (and the framing of the problem). Arriving at that knowledge requires two major changes on the part of many executives:

First, executives must commit to dedicating attention and time to deeply understanding the customer experience. That behavior represents a change because most executives operate at the 20,000-foot level. Second, and most important (because it's linked to the first change), they need to build trust. Unless creative team members trust the people offering critique, they will find it hard to hear (and believe) what they did wrong. Only a trusting creative team can hear that their work is bad without feeling as though *they* are bad.

THE VALUE OF CRITICISM

Art, architecture and design schools have always had a reputation for "tough love." Classes take place in a studio, which is a creative, dynamic and highly creative space. Most people who have gone through formal design training are passionate about their experiences in the studio. They talk fondly of endless critiques, long nights, and a few hours of sleep caught under their desks before the final review. The critique is what's particularly memorable about that studio experience and what drives so much reflection.

One of my colleagues, reflecting on a favorite professor, recalled a critique on a graphic-design printed piece. All of the students had put their work on the wall and were waiting for the professor to arrive. A few minutes past 9 a.m., the professor walked in. He looked at the wall for about 30 seconds. The students grew quiet. He turned and looked at them, slowly panning across the room to look into each student's eyes. He looked back at the wall, turned, and walked out of the room. The work was so bad that his critique was silence.

Another student, now a visual designer at frog, said that her most vivid memory of design school was "getting a D on my first project in Fundamentals of Design my freshman year. It was my first D ever—I cried in front of my professor and thought I needed to quit school."

This rough treatment isn't just fodder for funny stories. It helps students to understand the value of feedback and to thicken their skin. So it has immediate and practical value for these designers when they get into the harsh real world of the consultancy or corporation. In these environments, clients and creative directors don't pull punches or sugarcoat feedback; there's no time. Creative work becomes a point of departure for iterative revisions, so a thorough critique is the best outcome one can hope for. Detail that emerges during a negative design review brings valuable opportunities for corrections during subsequent revisions.

If you didn't go through some form of creativity education, you may have never experienced critique. In this section, I'll show you how to run a critique for your team, and how to get the most value out of this critical part of the process. Don't worry; you won't have to make people cry. You'll learn how to build trust with your team so that they can hear and absorb harsh criticism and still view you as their leader.

A CRITIQUE EXAMPLE

Critique happens throughout the entire creative process, starting with strategy. In this example, the product team is knee-deep in the execution of a new piece of software for our fictional education company. They are all gathered in the design studio looking at a wall pinned with pieces of paper. These papers show wireframe flows of a user's navigation.

As you read the critique, imagine that you are the creative director and project manager. Think about how you would drive a productive and useful conversation like this one.

> **Creative Director**: "Can you describe what's happening here?" [points at a wireframe showing large, bubbly letters and a number of vivid balloons and streamers]

> **Designer**: "Well, when the student finally picks a college major, I wanted to celebrate the choice by recognizing it as important; this element here [points to balloons] is congratulating them on choosing an academic plan."

> **Product Manager**: "That doesn't make any sense. Why make it a celebration? It's just one step on the long hard path of the academic journey. Wouldn't something more subtle be appropriate?"

> **Engineer**: "Yeah, I mean—this is education; it's not like a greeting-card company or something. It's not working at all. [in a mocking voice] 'Congratulations on your major—now you can pay the school hundreds of thousands of dollars!'"

> **Creative Director**: "It makes a lot of sense to overtly recognize that the user made a big decision because it will help them understand **state**—that they have moved from 'no major selected' to 'major selected'—and reinforce **personalization**. But is celebration really the right emotive quality?"

Designer: "Yeah, maybe not—I was trying to make it more happy to form a brand relationship."

Engineer: "But that relationship can come over time. It's not going to happen on this particular screen."

Designer: "OK, so if I keep the idea of recognition, but shift toward something less playful..."

Product Manager: "Yeah, save the playfulness for appropriate times, like maybe if they score well on a test, we give them a way to share it on Instagram. **That's** a celebration. Instead, let's put something here that directs the user back into the flow, so they can make additional tweaks to their course plan. This is an opportunity for us to sell 'course plan customization' to schools, too."

The critique is taking place in a conference room with a variety of participants. It's a dialogue, where the conversation flows from open-ended questioning ("Can you describe what's happening here?") to rationalization ("I was trying to make it...," "I wanted to...") to very detailed value judgments ("That doesn't make any sense," "That's not working at all"). The dialogue works for a number of reasons:

1. The designer is receptive to criticism but also has a chance to explain and justify creative decisions in a way that isn't defensive. This implies a power balance.

2. The creative director acts as a moderator—guiding the discussion through open-ended questions and continually summarizing—while also participating as a partial reviewer.

3. The relationship between the designer and the participants is not combative. We can assume that the group has a positive working relationship; otherwise, the designer would have seen the engineer's sarcastic comment as mean-spirited, and probably would have

ignored or combated it.

4. The viewed material has enough detail that the group can criticize thematic elements as well as detailed nuances. If the balloons were not drawn—if instead they were presented as boxes with the words "celebratory element"—this discussion would not have occurred. The artifact acts as the prompt, and the group reacts based on their experiences, the context of the problem, and the creative director's facilitation.

5. The critique is generative, meaning that it includes an idea for a new feature, rather than only responding to and honing existing product details. In this way, the artifact becomes the most important prompt.

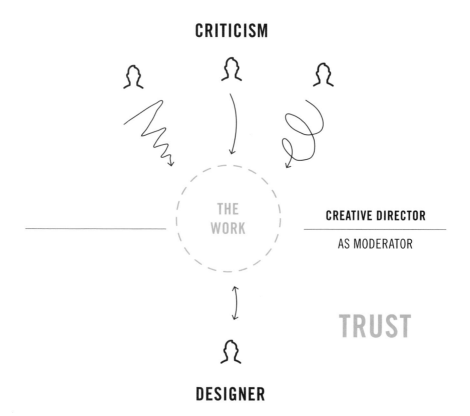

Ben Fullerton, Design Director at Nike Digital, describes the importance of authenticity in building trust in a critique. Without trust, creativity suffers. "You get designers receiving feedback that they don't necessarily value or trust, because they feel that it's not coming from a place of genuine interest in the work [but from] a place of basic misunderstanding about the work."

Fullerton says he believes his—and anyone's—role as a creative "leader and mentor is to make people I'm managing better than I ever was." For him, the way to accomplish that and build trust is to lead by example—making his own artifacts and encouraging criticism of them. Remaining hands-on is valuable for another reason: "At least, to be able to say to people, 'Look, this is the kind of thing I'm talking about,' and show how it could come to life; to use that as a sketch for them to go off and run with."

Of course being hands-on means keeping your creative skills up to date so you can make *good* artifacts and remain relevant. "Rough prototypes of how something could work; a bunch of sketches; some wireframes. Things that just get people to say, 'Oh, cool. I can pick this up and I can run with it. I know what I've got to do. This is a rough sketch of what I'm going to be doing. It's up to me to start to take that and make it better.'" (Fullerton, 2016) This may be different from how you think about a creative manager—in the thick of things, rather than on the sidelines.

LEARNING TO BE CRITIQUED

Although the example above was about software and at least one person who went to design school, the value of critique extends beyond digital products and designers. No matter what your level of corporate influence, your job is probably becoming more creative. Critique can help you with things that you might not think of as designed artifacts.

Think about all of the decisions you make each day. Nearly all of the big ones have a creative component: Are you planning to acquire a company? The acquisition process *creates* value. Are you planning to reorganize your company? You'll *create* the resulting structure. And that new go-to-market strategy? It's *created*—typically tied directly to the *creation* of a new product or service.

So, learning to critique and be critiqued is critical for advancing an idea. In a traditional corporate setting, it's up to you to demand critique and define the rules of engagement. Your teams probably won't understand what you are asking for. Explain that you actually want people to describe what isn't working. Then prepare to be open to hearing the bad news.

It won't be pretty. Most design students struggle through years of criticism before finding a confident voice and appetite for review. As a leader, you and your team will have to become comfortable without the forgiving safety of academia. But you'll find it worthwhile to do so because critique adds immense value to any part of the business—advancing or refining an idea and ensuring that quality work gets the attention it deserves.

A negative but structured design critique helps people learn that creativity is not entirely subjective or about beauty or the eye of the beholder. Particularly in a strategic sense, creativity has rigor, structure, and method. Even preparing for the critique forces that rigor because there has to be an artifact to critique.

RUNNING THE CRITIQUE

The actual mechanics of a critique seem simple. A group discusses a displayed artifact and explore suggestions for improvement. Printed out or projected, the artifact can represent an idea, a strategy, or a tactic. It can represent a simple feature or a series of function vignettes. You can critique anything you can embody in an artifact, including brand campaigns, microsites, products, services, business models, and organizational plans.

The "group" part of the critique is essential because of the goal of a critique: to extract as much content as possible. Multiple viewpoints—particularly competing ones—best serve that goal.

What's also essential is explicitly stating the rules for the critique. Tell the group how you want to run it and how you want them to participate:

First, because the intent is to identify problems, ask your team to focus on the negative. This runs counter to normal behavior—many of us were taught that "if you can't say anything nice, don't say anything at all." So you can expect to feel a strange dynamic in the room. Think about the power dynamics at play in any meeting where you have a title that conveys expectations of authority or expertise. You need to explicitly reset those expectations: "You may view me as the de facto expert on this topic or feel too intimidated to offer negative criticism. For the purposes of this meeting, consider me just another contributor. I *want* you to identify problems with my solution."

Next, instruct the team to constructively present negative comments—not just to say what's wrong but to give very specific suggestions on how to improve it. Tell them that for each comment they make about something not working, they need to explain how to fix it.

Explain that you want to focus the criticism on the artifact—the *representation* of the idea—not the idea itself. The artifact both represents the idea (or strategy) and grounds it in reality. That grounding tends to enable a specific conversation, so the team can say "this, not that." If the conversation drifts into the theoretical realm, though, it's up to you to reground the conversation in specifics.

Most important, urge the team to sketch solutions whenever possible. Explain that you'll give the marker to the person speaking, and that you'll constantly prompt drawn comments. If you are critiquing an organizational diagram on a PowerPoint slide, print the slide and sketch directly on that piece of paper. If it's a business model, redraw it in real time on the whiteboard. Recognize that some people are not comfortable drawing in real time, though, and that you may need to draw for them.

Having established the rules, begin the critique. As the critique starts, resist the temptation to rationalize your decisions. This will always come across as defensive because it is. And that defensiveness changes the conversation from a way to produce new knowledge to a verbal debate that prohibits idea evolution.

Additionally, when you rationalize particular creative decisions during a critique, you steer the conversation in two ways:

- You call attention to a particular element, at the expense of the whole (and prime the group to be thinking mostly of that particular item), and

- You set up a boundary around your choice and implicitly claimed ownership over it. Some people might refuse to cross the boundary once you've publicly established it. You've signaled, "I care about this, and if you poke at it, you'll hurt my feelings." In fact, you *may* have called attention to the element you care most about!

So if you aren't supposed to rationalize and defend your work, what *are* you supposed to do?

Transition the group to the critique—"Let's get started. Who would like to begin?" Then be quiet, and take notes. Speak only to remind the team to keep talking and to draw.

Some of the best parts of a critique come from small, nuanced details and the many ideas that the conversation sparks so taking notes and saving sketches is vital to retain them. For example, a participant who is looking at an Excel model of an acquisition strategy might say something like, "When we describe acquiring these companies over here, instead of treating them like a 'rollup,' it seems like we could 'sunset' three of the products and focus on moving customers towards the fourth. Then we could slowly increase the price of the core product and provide ancillary benefit from our services group."

There are at least four suggestions there—sunsetting products, consolidating customers, increasing prices, and engaging the services group. Without notes and sketches, it's unlikely that you would remember all of that or a part because you'll be actively considering so many ideas.

During critiques of my work, I take notes on my laptop, and I sketch on a stack of paper. I number each item, component, or artifact on both the paper and in the typed notes. As a person is speaking, I try to type the exact comment and link to its number. I also try to log who said what, so I can follow up later if I need to. In a few instances, I've found written feedback to be *politically* useful, too: When teams wonder where seemingly irrelevant decisions came from, we can identify who hatched them.

A critique can feel overwhelming because it can generate a large quantity of comments, suggestions, and complaints. As a group gains momentum and sometimes seems to rip apart your core idea, you'll again be tempted to defend your work. Instead consider that those comments and your recording of them don't mean you have to act on them. It should be liberating to recognizing that a critique is not a mandate and that comments are only suggestions.

The end of a creative meeting is just as important as its beginning and center. People tend to leave the critique with very different views about what happened. If you quietly listened and took notes, one view they're likely to share is validation—that you heard them. That builds and reinforces trust and teamwork.

But be warned: Because the participants talked and drew their ideas into existence and saw you paying attention, they will come to think of their ideas as facts. If they don't see them reflected in the next round of revisions, you'll frustrate them. They'll feel as though you ignored them and they wasted their time.

To prevent this reaction, also set ground rules at the end of the critique: Explain how the post-critique synthesis will work. Say something like, "I heard all of what you said, and I wrote it all down. You've given me a lot to think about. I don't agree with everything, so you may not see your comments visualized in the next iteration. If you feel strongly about what you said today, let's talk about it in a one-on-one setting."

If you're in a big or politically volatile group, email everyone both your notes and this disclaimer: "These notes represent what was said during the critique, not what was committed to." Then, no matter how strongly you emphasize the value your future work, be prepared to explain why you choose to ignore specific design suggestions.

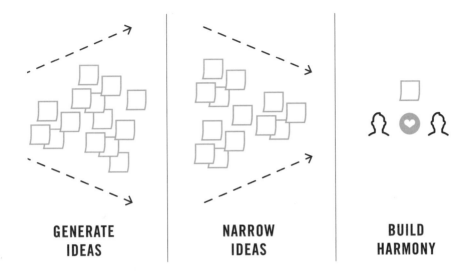

| GENERATE IDEAS | NARROW IDEAS | BUILD HARMONY |

To recap the importance and role of a critique—

It generates many ideas. It helps you escape the typical blind spot of an expert and see things in a new light. In expanding the canvas of potential, it also expands your solution set.

It acts as a way to narrow, refine, and improve the ideas you already came up with. It focuses and sharpens the solution set.

It builds comfort among the team by helping to manage the creative ambiguity and anxiety around a new idea. That's because the critique shares the idea—it now belongs to the team, no longer only you. Because team members own it, they will support it, align around it, and champion it through the rest of the process.

HOLD CRITIQUES REGULARLY, AND BE SURE TO ARTICULATE AND ENFORCE THEIR RULES TO ENSURE THE PRODUCTIVE TRANSMISSION OF NEGATIVE CRITICISM.

CHAPTER 6

BUILDING A CREATIVE CULTURE

When I was 8, I took a class in wheel-thrown ceramics. On the first day of class, my teacher made a beautiful two-foot-tall vase and sliced it in half, lengthwise. Imagine, a perfect form, ruined on purpose. I was astounded— and jealous. I couldn't make anything even close to that, and there he was, ruining it on purpose! He said it was to show us how thick it was. Later, I realized it was to show impermanence. He wanted us to learn that when you get good at making things, the things themselves stop being precious.

Much later, as an 18-year-old design student at Carnegie Mellon, I learned another valuable lesson in *making*. It was my first semester and my first critique of my first assignment: a hand-drawn self-portrait. The results were up on the wall. Mine was *awful,* far and away the worst thing on display. It was out of proportion and had poor line weight—even poor paper stock. The only things going for it were marks so soft and tentative that no one could really even see it. My face was burning red, and I was sitting as far back in the studio as I could get, trying to make myself as small as possible. Although I already knew the need to make things to find a solution, I was embarrassed that my execution was so removed from my vision.

In both examples, I was struck by the relationship between making things and feelings. When my ceramics teacher cut the vase in half, I felt jealousy and shame. During the critique at school, I again felt shame that because my work wasn't good, *I* wasn't good. For many people, what drives such self-criticism is perceiving the gap between their work and their taste, according to Ira Glass, host of National Public Radio's *This American Life:* "All of us who do creative work, we get into it because we have good taste. For the first couple years, you make stuff, and it's just not that good. But your taste, the thing that got you into the game, is still killer. And your taste is why your work disappoints you." (Gianatasio, 2015)

That mismatch comes to life in the creation of an artifact. The creative process is, abstractly, about conceiving of things that didn't yet exist, and then actually making them exist. When I was a creative director, one of my favorite things to hear in the office was, "Well, I made a thing." It's often a declaration of achievement, but just as often, you hear a tone of frustration, as in, "Well, I made a thing. But it's not very good."

When you make a thing and inject a little bit of your essence and your feelings into it, you're vulnerable. There you are, showing these feelings to anyone who wanders by, and waiting to hear their reactions. Putting yourself in that vulnerable position requires absolute trust. When junior staff members make something, doing so can open a giant space of introspection. What often fills that space is an emotional churn similar to what I experienced in my clay and drawing classes. The thing they make becomes a placeholder for all sorts of *other* things: Aspirations. Self-deprecation. Anger.

These emotions are weird things to talk about in a business context. As managers, we're not therapists. Work is supposed to be professional, and emotion isn't welcome in the traditional workplace. But it finds its way in, particularly in a high-profile creative setting. The more a company believes in creativity, the more it shines a light on the output. And when that happens, designers realize their limitations. This realization introduces emotion into the workplace in a way that's no longer hidden.

In a creative organization, emotions run wild. At the same time that the made thing causes the designer's emotional self-critique, the thing prompts critique from others, exerting additional emotional pressure.

Let's take a look at emotions in the workplace, and how they often get in the way of driving creative vision.

UNDERSTANDING EMOTIONS
IN THE WORKPLACE

Imagine the most conservative environment you can think of—a company or organization that you would never, ever describe as creative. It's likely that you thought of the U.S. government, which we typically describe as massive, slow moving, and overly bureaucratic.

Embedded in that conservative environment, Stephanie Wade was the Director of the Innovation Lab at the United States Office of Personnel Management (OPM). The lab's mission is to introduce creativity to various government agencies and the White House. The lab's *goals* are to help government employees understand the role of creativity in dealing with large-scale social problems and to help organizations think differently about these problems. Wade and her team built the lab, modeled on an education consultancy, upon three core pillars.

The first pillar was that the group would be subject-matter experts in creativity and design innovation within government. This meant hiring and building a unique skillset—bringing in strategic visual thinkers who would solve problems in unique ways. This pillar was about building a culture of problem framing, critique, and ideation.

The second pillar was to serve as teachers—training government workers to apply a creative approach to solving challenging issues. This pillar was a way of spreading the culture, language, and skills of creativity through government.

The third pillar was to directly take on the wicked problems facing government, and use a creative approach to solve them. One of the lab's early projects—a litmus test for the pillar—centered around the National School

Lunch Program of the United States Department of Agriculture (USDA).

The program provides discounted or free meals to students who are unable to afford lunch on their own through payments to schools.

Internally, the organization knew that the program was plagued by un-documented, inaccurate, misdirected, and misused payments. The program had a 15% error rate, higher than other government programs, including unemployment insurance, Medicaid, Medicare, and rental housing (Pacifico, 2016). The lab partnered with USDA's Food and Nutrition Services to address these improper payments. Instead of performing traditional audits, such as reviewing documents and payment processes, Wade's team lever-aged the design-thinking process to better understand the school-lunch landscape.

The team conducted qualitative research with the process' constituents. "We talked to the school-lunch ladies and the principals, and we watched the kids in the program go through the process." The research revealed one of the biggest problems: the four-page paper application that parents of pro-gram recipients must fill out every year. It was a problem because, "...it felt like it was written for someone with a PhD in government. It wasn't written for the audience, which are low income, and English is most likely not their first language. They have poor reading and writing skills... The application error rate was very high, and to compensate, schools were organizing events at night to help the parents fill out the application correctly." (Wade, 2017)

The application included instructions similar to a tax form, with compound logical if/then statements:

"IF NO ONE IN YOUR HOUSEHOLD GETS STATE SUPPLEMENTAL NUTRITION ASSISTANCE PROGRAM (SNAP), OR TEMPORARY ASSSISTANCE FOR NEEDY

FAMILIES (TANF) BENEFITS AND IF ANY CHILD IN YOUR HOUSEHOLD IS HOMELESS, A MIGRANT OR RUNAWAY, FOLLOW THESE INSTRUCTIONS."

The application even contained circular references to the form itself ("Part 4: Complete only if a child in your household isn't eligible under Part 3. See instructions for All Other Households"). (USDA, 2015)

The team linked much of the waste of millions of dollars per year to the fact that parents were inaccurately filling out the form. Then they set to the task of finding a solution—one of the first times a design-thinking approach was leveraged in the government. The challenges in finding the solution, the team found, weren't about the actual design problem of making the application form easier to understand. They were about the emotional and cultural changes necessary to implement a creative process.

Wade further describes those some of those challenges and how her team addressed them.

1. **Team members were skeptical of a new, creative process.** They were made up of both existing government employees and new hires with a design background. The existing government employees lacked confidence in the creative process—including qualitative research, ideation, and idea generation—because they hadn't seen it work. They questioned, and often didn't trust, that their efforts would lead to a success.

   This is a common worry because, as we've seen, the creative process feels (and often is) fuzzy and subjective. As we've also seen, the goal of a creative engagement can be poorly defined, and the process itself generates constraints that, in turn, provide clarity. For team members who had never completed the process, the methodology was difficult to embrace and skepticism was difficult to suspend.

To address this problem, the team's designers created a training curriculum for other team members at the same time as the team pursued the USDA program work. The workplace became an environment for learning, not just doing. The team also reapplied this set of educational materials to share outside the team.

2. **Team members were unable to see alternative, creative solutions to an existing problem.** Many had been working on the school-lunch program for more than a decade so they were entrenched in their view of the problem. They were experts in improper payments, so they framed the problem based around what they knew rather than in new ways. That's the expert's blind spot I mentioned in the previous chapter.

   To shift this entrenched perspective, the team focused on quick iterations built on user feedback. The team, Wade explained, "would play around with ideas, and then approach random people on the streets to test them." By leaving the building, they were able to generate anecdotes about the work and bring evidence of successful progress to drive future iterations. And by building empathy with non-experts during real-world qualitative research, team members could see new problem frames.

3. **The team was skeptical of a new process being introduced into the organization, driven by a new leader.** Wade's background was in creative consulting, not in government. And, typical of the attitude toward any new leader in an organization, there was fear about how she would adapt to the culture or attempt to change it.

   Wade mitigated this feeling of distrust by participating as a hands-on leader, doing the creative work alongside the team. She developed a "we're all in this together" demeanor that built a feeling of comradery and trust. This hands-on approach required tradeoffs with her management work. "To manage my workload, I put a line in the sand. I'm doing x hours with my project team, and x on the operations side, and something will get sacrificed. I protected that, so I could be there with the team in a real way."

4. **Perhaps most important, the culture of creativity initially established an "us versus them" atmosphere.** The new creative staff was viewed as shiny and new, and it seemed at times that they were leaving behind the people that had been working on the problem for years. To champion creativity, Wade says, the designers "wore that rebel cape on the outside. But that rebel nature alienates us from who we are trying to win over."

To be inclusive, designers became more aware of their language. "We tried not using the traditional design language I had learned. I made it colloquial." Common language made the new approaches more accessible and made new techniques feel familiar and less strange.

The problems Wade experienced and addressed all stem from two cultures colliding. Almost by definition, government is slow. Checks and balances ensure the discussion of controversial ideas and the mitigation of risks. By introducing and embracing creativity, Wade encouraged the team to move fast and take risks. "A creative culture," she says, "means daring them to come up with crazy ideas." More than anything else, establishing trust is key to introducing the creative process into a conservative environment like the U.S. government.

Establishing trust is also fundamental for introducing creativity into any other organization. Trust enables team members to depend on one another to do what's right, and to operate from the same point of mission and toward the best (and shared) interests of the company. Those are often also major goals of team-building retreats and corporate-mission-alignment meetings. Team-building activities are often about showing one's vulnerability, so that team members can relate to one another on an emotional, human level.

Creative trust focuses on understanding the way to offer and deliver criticism, and how to receive and react to a creative deliverable. When working on the USDA project, Wade identified that the delivery and receipt of criticism required meaningful creative trust. She explains, "when you develop or create something, it feels so great. It can be a new graphic image, a sketch, it feels exhilarating and it's a part of yourself. And when you put a part of yourself on display at work, to be critiqued in a vulnerable way, it's sacred. How you handle that artifact, that manifestation of creativity. It is really important to treat that in a way that's respectful and values the team's work, their creativity."

Many of our traditional and conservative organizations have cultures similar to those of the government. Those cultures don't include making or critiquing, so employees don't understand how to react to the artifacts. And that lack of understanding can cause introversion: "In that type of environment, I know that when I put it out there, they don't know how to handle it with kid gloves. It makes me not trust them to handle it the way I want... I don't trust them to critique it." Wade isn't saying here that she worries about receiving a negative critique. She's saying that she worries about receiving a *wrong*, or *inappropriate* critique, such as "I don't like it" or "That will never work."

And so, in addition to training the team and the entire organization in design, Wade also had to train them in how to react to creative deliverables.

Critique, in this context, means to identify something good to build towards new ideas. Her technique is to "start with the good." But, she said, that's not what she learned in grad school. "...I was taught to find the weakness because it meant I was smarter. Focusing on the good is never wrong, and it's never insincere. There's always some point of magical goodness in something, some element of beauty, of hitting the mark. Focus on that, and figure out how to build on that to focus on the next iteration."

Over time, Wade and her team were able to establish a culture of trust that brought together disparate perspectives to function effectively. Her teams were able to embrace criticism as a fundamental part of the creative process and to shepherd ideas through a creative engine with ease. Their empathetic journey into the school-lunch program included working with users and proposing ideas that seemed outlandish or unrealistic. It resulted in a redesigned application of a single page.

According to USDA's Jeff Greenfield, the office responsible for the program "...has credited the lab and its design process with changing how we approach problem solving." (Kalil, 2015) The success of the program, and the lessons learned, have shifted the entire way this government organization approaches creativity.

TRAIN THE ORGANIZATION NOT JUST IN THE METHOD OF CRITIQUE, BUT ALSO IN THE CULTURE OF CREATIVITY AND THE NEED FOR TRUST.

THE ELEMENTS OF A CREATIVE CULTURE

When we think of creative companies, we often picture Nerf darts and bean bags, and we associate creativity with sexy consumer companies like Facebook or Apple. But you can find creativity in some unlikely places, like government, as we've just seen. You can even find it in industries like finance and banking, as is the case of Earnest, a midsized startup that promises to "offer better student loan rates through deeper data analysis, as well as unrivaled flexibility and client support." (Earnest, 2017)

Earnest has taken a creative and modern approach to student loans. The company has been tremendously successful, having raised close to $300 million and having grown from 30 to 160 employees in a little less than two years. The company lends between $2 million and $5 million per day, with an average loan of $70,000. (Shieber, 2015)

The business approves student loans based on applicants' behavioral data—assets, liabilities, spending patterns, and bank-account contents—rather than credit score. A fair amount of this data comes directly from those bank accounts, which applicants link to Earnest.

The company has a simple cultural formula that has helped them remain creative. They view themselves primarily as a technology company rather than a financial company. According to Brian Romanko, CTO of Earnest, "a characteristic of being a creative technology company is that one of your competitive advantages should be cost. And humans cost way more than computers do. We wanted to have all of the product pillars represented very early on—product, design, engineering and data science. Those were the roles we hired first; we didn't actually hire people into credit operations and loan processors until we had loan applications. We were underwriting the loans ourselves." The team celebrated creators rather than those in management or operations, and this translated to hiring behavior.

The big idea for Earnest came directly from its CEO, Louis Beryl, whose own student-loan applications were declined. Romanko explains, "…[Beryl] was like, 'This is crazy. I know that I'm financially responsible. I know that I've paid all my debt obligations. I know that I'm going to Harvard. I'm going to be highly employable when I finish this program.' He had to get his mom to co-sign with him. It just made no sense. So we started looking into how these determinations are made, and we found that nearly everyone uses credit scores. And credit scores have very coarse data. The majority of the data that goes into those algorithms comes from your debt obligations. And the frequency at which data is updated is essentially monthly."

The team recognized that people have attributes that credit scores don't track. Applicants have assets, education, and employment, which those algorithms didn't account for. So the seed of the company was a hypothesis that they could build a risk profile that takes into account those other characteristics, and the profile would be more accurate than a normal credit score. They looked to tools like LinkedIn to identify education and employment data, school records to prove enrollment, and a bank account to prove financial stability.

Romanko continues, "People thought we were crazy when we told them, 'Oh, we're going to get people to link their bank accounts to go through our loan application process.' But by connecting that account, we can see the stream of transactional data. It's at a daily frequency as opposed to a monthly frequency. And we see inflows and outflows. We can see your 401(k) account. We can see your savings account. So we can get this complete financial picture."

The company's hypothesis proved to be correct. They found that millennials—their target audience—were willing to connect their bank-account information if it gave them a lower loan rate, and it did. And the rate varies from borrower to borrower. The company bases individual loan terms on each user's data and experiences.

The CEO came up with the key innovation of linking a bank account, and the leadership team established the company's vision. That vision, a clear north star, established a culture of technology first throughout the company. For example, as the company was exploring student-loan refinancing, one of Earnest's data scientists identified the traditional step-function pricing as an ineffective way of treating loans.

Romanko recalls an email exchange with that employee, who wrote, "If you've got a 5-year loan that costs $1,000 a month and a 10-year loan that costs $500 a month, and your budget is $750, you have no choice but to take the longer loan. And what ends up happening there is that your loan duration is longer, and you're actually paying more in interest than you would have otherwise.... it's not fair to the borrower that you're collecting this additional interest."

Through more emails between the executive and the contributor, the pair arrived at a feature called precision pricing, where a user could actually set the loan budget. Earnest could then offer a loan with specific "non-standard" terms to that user, such as a seven-and-a-half year loan at a unique rate.

The idea that innovation can come from the bottom up is fundamental to a creative culture. It means that employees feel safe and empowered, and feel a sense of ownership over the company's products and services. They don't view their job as simply a way to earn a paycheck. Instead, they view it as something to shape and mold, something that they have control over. The employee who helped to develop the successful feature had influence that the company developed as an explicit focus.

Although most companies now use technology to deliver products and services, being a creative technology company has a key indicator, Romanko explains. The company invests in developing technology instead of being constrained by trying to integrate off-the-shelf solutions. The company trusts the technology teams. "The amount of influence that those people (technologists, designers, and product managers) have," he says, "is equal or possibly greater than the influence of the business or operational teams, and that makes a big difference. If the organization is purely people who don't come from a creative technology background, they're going to view the company from a sort of mechanical perspective, centered around a balance-sheet view."

Additionally, the company has a culture of humility, so employees feel em-powered to push back on leadership. Even interns have openly challenged the CEO in all-hands meetings, "Positional authority was never something that people paid attention to." The company reinforces this culture through a variety of tactics; for example, all of their GitHub source code reposito-ries are open to the company, and anyone can create a pull request (which means that anyone can essentially add their own content to the products). As a result, even non-technical users can make copy changes directly to the things customers see.

Additionally, in the early days of the company, Romanko says, they rotated desks every few months, to maintain a culture of openness. "One month, you might be sitting next to a client-happiness person. The next month, you're sitting next to a finance person. We did this until we were 50 people. The other intent was—[you] don't get the window seat because you've worked at Earnest forever. That wasn't something we wanted. We wanted people who felt comfortable and could interact with other teams."

Finally, the company has a culture of hard work and focus on products. It is clear on hiring people who are cultural fits with the company. Although the team has fun, it has no stocked liquor cabinets, bean bags, or foosball tables. The culture may be a result of the age of the founders, Romanko notes, "We were all sort of mid-30s folks... it just wasn't our personality, so it didn't end up in the culture."

CEO Beryl explains that this culture is fundamental to the success of a creative company: "It's not just about previous experience or technical skills. More important is the culture fit of the team: Does everyone work well together, does each member have the passion to solve this particular problem, survive the ups and downs of an early stage startup and do whatever it takes to be successful?" (Beryl, 2014)

From Earnest, we can learn a few key lessons.

- First, they view themselves as a creative technology company, and so they invest in technologists and technology. When Romanko's team considers a problem, they try to improve the problem through computation, not through warm bodies. This seems obvious, but large companies often ignore the core infrastructure of their products and see large teams as more important than good products. At Earnest, they prioritize hiring creators, rather than operations staff, and they attempt to minimize operational overhead through automation, technological advancement, and process improvements.

- Next, the team at Earnest intentionally creates an environment where new ideas can come either from executive leadership or from individual contributors. They foster this environment through open meetings, transparent decision-making, and collaborative creativity, as is the case with GitHub additions. Bottom-up ideas are treated as first-class citizens, as important as mandates that come from the top. As a result, employees feel empowered to offer new ideas and try new things.

- Employees are also empowered to speak their mind, and even to publicly disagree with executives. This means no negative repercussions to this type of disagreement, and more important, the company can track positive action (like the adoption of a new feature) directly to the interaction between an executive and an employee. This form of openness creates a flat organizational mindset, so employees feel ownership around the company's products and services.

- Finally, the team's culture is built around hard work and quality products, not around typical indicators of fun; the team's demeanor is mature, and specific culture-fit hiring criteria reinforce that maturity. Rather than emphasizing traditional cultural icons of a technology company (like foosball tables or free lunches), the company emphasizes shipping great products and taking pride in a job well done.

There's a connection between what we've seen in the government—through OPM—and at Earnest. Both organizations developed a creative culture based on trust: Leaders identified the fundamentals of openness, encouragement, and direct input and did their best to foster these ideas. While these ideas were shaped and refined somewhat organically over time, they were initially the result of explicit focus on culture. A creative culture comes by design and shouldn't be left to circumstance.

ESTABLISH TRUST AS A FUNDAMENTAL COMPANY PILLAR BY PRIORITIZING CREATIVE HIRES AND MAKING IT CLEAR THAT EMPLOYEES CAN CRITIQUE IDEAS, CHALLENGE LEADERSHIP, AND EXPLORE THROUGH MAKING.

ENCOURAGING AUTONOMY IN STRATEGIC DECISION MAKING

When I first joined frog design, a global innovation firm, my role was as an individual creative contributor. I was responsible for making things that helped clients better understand the business problems they faced, and offering creative solutions to those problems. My second project at frog was for a big telecom client. The small team I was on had been camped out in a conference room for several weeks working on an important deliverable. The work was good, and as we got closer and closer to the deadline, our team felt better and better about what we were delivering—not that we were the ones delivering it.

In a consultancy like frog, senior roles usually take on more client-facing tasks. Designers may *do* the work, but a creative director will present and explain that work to the client. Often, that creative director won't be aware of all of the detailed design decisions that happen along the way. So there's an awkward handoff when the director takes the work, gets on a plane, and everyone waits nervously for the report about how the meeting went.

We finished that telecom project on a Thursday, around 8pm. We had a solid design, a solid story around the design, and we had spent several hours helping Patrick, our creative director, to understand how to best present the materials. We wished him good luck, and he flew to San Jose for the meeting.

The next afternoon, Patrick called to say that the meeting had gone well, the client was happy, and we were likely to get some follow-on work. He said he was really proud of the work, then mentioned in an offhand way that he made some changes that seemed to help the story.

When Patrick showed us the final presentation and design work, it looked nothing like what we had made. He had scrapped 75% of the story we were telling. Our work was still there, but the frame of the work had changed. The hours we had spent arguing over details and agonizing over decisions went down the drain, and we were devastated. I was extremely upset because I felt personally slighted. Red hot, I unloaded on him.

He listened, and when I was done, he calmly explained that he really, really liked our work. In his view, it was tactically great (it was executed well, had wonderful craft, and looked beautiful). But based on his experience with the client, he knew it wouldn't go over well because it didn't tell the right story. He walked me through changes, explaining why he made them.

I still left mad, vowing to never redo someone's work—to never sit on a plane and blow away weeks and weeks of creativity. And yet, years later, in the role of design leader, I found myself doing just that. I saw that the work my team had produced wasn't ready for presentation. My experience told me that it wouldn't resonate because that the narrative wasn't clear. And the only thing I could do was redo it, quickly, before the meeting. I knew how the designer would feel, and I knew the kind of credibility I would lose. I also knew it was on me because I should have intervened weeks before.

By changing our work, Patrick undermined the team's efforts. By doing so without telling us, he lost our trust. But had he not changed the work, we probably would have lost the account. And I repeated all of those actions when I was in a position to think both strategically and tactically.

While there are important morals in this story about trust and rework, one of the most important takeaways lies in the difference between working tactically (making things) and working strategically (telling a story). Where Patrick and I redid the team's work, it was because the artifacts didn't speak for themselves: they needed a persuasive backstory. We identified the need for the backstory only when the work was done, and consequently, we redid the strategic context of the work only after the completion of tactical work.

If I had been embedded with the team the entire length of the project, I would have had as much ownership to the creative output as they did, and the strategic framing would have become apparent earlier. I could have led the team towards the correct frame, or they would have found their way there on their own.

Mark Rolston, former Chief Creative Officer at frog, has insight into this type of dual thinking: strategic storytelling and tactical artifact creation. He describes the difference between creative-directing a small group—as at his new firm Argo—and the giant creative team of more than 300 creative professionals that he managed at frog design:

As a creative leader in a small team, Rolston explains, you are, and should be, directly involved in the creative process. But when you have such a hands-on role, he says, creative direction can run the risk of being too prescriptive. A creative staff literally translates what you say and do, and it's tempting to fall into a trap of do-as-I-say. The staff is "simply saying 'now what?' And you find yourself saying, 'make that smaller. Smaller.' You might as well pick up the mouse and do it yourself."

However, Rolston, adds, a small team affords the ability for more regular check-ins, so critique becomes both serendipitous (it could happen at any time) and regular (it happens all the time). With a small group, it's easier to maintain a flat organization, which builds trust and empowers people to take more ownership and control. "People know each other and can self-organize." That self-organization means more opportunities for connection between people and between work.

Critique in such a small team becomes more frequent, as it's a simple act of walking around the room and seeing what people are doing. "I realized over 30 years of doing this that by showing up at someone's desk, and saying 'show me what you got'—you create a sense that I could be there any time, and your work product should maintain velocity and your thinking should maintain enough fidelity that you can talk about the work." For Rolston, impromptu critiques mean that everyone is always ready. They'll be more prepared to draw, and hear things that appear and feel negative.

Compare that culture of intimacy to what happens in a much larger creative organization. At scale, the tactics of top-down criticism become more difficult. Sure, an executive can wander around, but with hundreds of staff, it becomes impractical to be aware of each person's work (and it can be scary for the person who is suddenly under the scrutiny of an executive high up in the corporate food chain). So the critiquing emphasis switches from tiny details to underlying ideas.

In that large company, Rolston says, your goal is to shape organizational values that the team then translates into actions. "You are moving minds very abstractly through a set of objectives." At frog, he organized a group of executive creative directors and gave them each a center of gravity, such as "health care" or "education," rather than just management of specific products or clients. They were then empowered to be the internal spokesman for that area.

"By keeping the vague notion they are in charge of that area, but they don't have a division called 'education' where they are responsible for their own P&L; they are the intellectual mascot for that topic." This gives them authority and a voice for creative leadership, but minimizes some of the more traditional managerial problems, like fighting for scarce resources or thinking narrowly about a solution. (Rolston, 2016)

When Rolston was in charge of such a large group, he made it feel smaller by dividing it into these focus areas, so that they could move quickly. Managing a large creative team has huge challenges, and many creative leaders point to small teams as being foundational to their success. Jeff Bezos, Founder of Amazon, developed the "two-pizza team" rule, saying that the ideal team can be fed with two pizzas or less. The size reflects an organizational philosophy of self-governance and independence. Each team can work in their own way, at their own pace, and with their own goals in mind. For creative people, this autonomy is a fundamental.

As the former lead in Dell's Experience Design Group, Kevin McDonald was in charge of driving uniformity across pre-installed software products. Before his team's work, software at Dell was, as he described, "kind of like a real ugly stepchild. You would open up your new computer and it looked like NASCAR, with virus scanners, random software—whoever would pay the most to have their software on the computer ended up on the desktop."

McDonald's group was positioned as a small, independent unit intended to fix that pervasive problem. "We were this ninja organization in this large, moribund enterprise. Our team's culture was very much insulated. Not a lot of people were paying attention to what we were doing. We were in this little room away from everyone, where we built a little headquarters. We took over a conference room. There was a sense of ownership there." Each member of the team was able to understand and see the strategy, and see how their work contributed to it. The physical isolation of the team had a tradeoff, though. The larger company and other stakeholders didn't know what was happening.

The strategic organization at Airbnb is similar. Joe Gebbia, Co-Founder and Chief Product Officer, says that his leadership team goes out of its way to keep creative teams connected. "As your organization grows bigger, you have to work very hard to keep design and development close together.

There's a natural inertia that wants to separate those two things… It's important to us to keep those circles as close together as possible. It influences how we lay out the office, how we structure out meetings, how we socialize with each other, and how we share information and insights. We try to cohabitate as much as we can, which is hard, because as teams evolve, they get more specialized. The more specialized you get, the further apart things become." (Gebbia, 2013)

Each of the creative leaders described above embraced creativity in small, insular teams because the teams were able to gain autonomy into their creative work: They pushed the creative culture down to the individual contributors, so they could work both strategically and tactically. They had autonomy, and in that autonomy comes control. Small teams can move quickly, can make decisions on their own, and can continue to drive iterations at a high velocity. They don't need to stop their flow of iteration/critique; this can happen naturally, and continually.

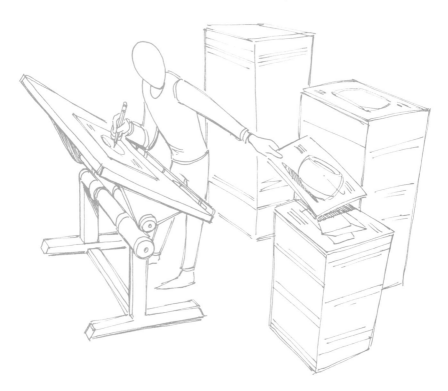

BUILD SMALL TEAMS AND EMPOWER THEM TO MAKE AUTONOMOUS DECISIONS AND RETAIN AUTONOMOUS CONTROL.

GAINING CONFIDENCE THROUGH OWNERSHIP

People talk a lot about "owning" a product, and that has several meanings. Ownership could mean responsibility for the process—being the individual who has their butt on the line if something goes wrong or if the product isn't delivered according to plan. That type of ownership focuses on results, and typically means the person will have to steer the ship in the right direction. Ownership could also mean being supportive and owning the ability for the team to deliver. It's a subtle difference, but it's one focused on mentorship and guidance, with the implicit belief that a good, happy team will reach the finish line with the right thing at the right time.

A third form of ownership refers to the features of the product or service itself. In this model, the "product owner" makes the decisions about the actual design. They have final approval on what gets built, and why it gets built. The expectation is that this person has more knowledge, more skill, and more vision than the rest of the team, and that they need to set a course for the product's vision, not only its execution.

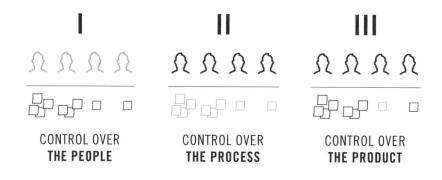

I	II	III
CONTROL OVER **THE PEOPLE**	CONTROL OVER **THE PROCESS**	CONTROL OVER **THE PRODUCT**

The last model is often disparaged in business books. It's considered arrogant; consider the old adage, "there's no 'I' in team." But this last model works. Some people *are* more experienced, *do* have more refined skills, and *do* have vision and drive. When a project has a clearly articulated and competent leader, a team performs really, really well. It's fulfilling to follow a leader with a vision, and if you agree with the vision, it feels empowering. You have a reason to go to work.

If you are that leader of that group, it's exhilarating to have a team of people following you and believing in you, and that belief helps reinforce the direction. It helps you double down on your decision with weird circular logic—"I can't be wrong because all of these people are following me—because they think I'm not wrong..."

But this model has an important caveat: It doesn't work if the leader has a track record of being wrong. I once worked for a CEO who made promises he didn't keep, and when he asked me to work for him again at another company, I ran as fast as I could in the opposite direction—once bitten, twice shy. After watching him fail, I was much more aware of his negative leadership traits; I felt misled.

The autocratic vision also doesn't work if the leader isn't charismatic because people *don't* want to follow them. Decisions become full of friction, back-channel rumors weighs down the team, trust erodes, and people quit. It's hard to lead a team that doesn't exist.

Charisma is baked into a personality, but it also can be learned with experience. You can learn things like tone, language, and the appropriate place and time to make demands and give instruction. You can learn from mistakes. For example, early on I let a conversation turn into a near-shouting match in a public space at work. I've never done that again because I learned to be aware of my tone of voice and the unproductive and downright-mean nature of such an interaction. I didn't have enough experience to know those things, and most young designers don't either.

Such situations are perhaps the biggest problem with the "lone leader" model. In many companies, a creative team member is handed a problem and told, "You need to own this." They often hear, "You need to have a vision, know all the answers, and make sure everyone does what you say." And that's recipe for disaster. In consultancies, when senior creatives get promoted to associate creative director, their demeanor can change overnight. They feel a responsibility to be seen as strong, which often translates into overbearing.

I just watched this happen to a member of my staff at my previous company. Ted, about four years into his career, demonstrated the same overbearing behavior when he received a small project to run and I told him he was the "project leader." I chose those words to see how he would grow into the idea of leadership. On conference calls, he would mandate how things would be, and when people asked questions, he would shut them down. In critique, he didn't explain his decision-making; he proactively and loudly defended his decisions, rather than explain them. When he interacted with engineers, he treated them like hired help rather than team members. In all, he turned into someone he wasn't, and he wasn't fun to be around.

After a few weeks, I mentioned to Ted that I had seen his behavior change, and I asked why he was coming across so defensive. He looked at me and said, "You said I was the leader. So I was trying to lead."

Ted had seen leaders get results, and in the face of complexity, a seemingly quick path to results is to force them. But that approach ignores the complexity of a creative environment in which people have good ideas and don't like being told what to do. He assumed there was only one way to lead because he had seen only the outputs of leadership—success or failure.

But there are many ways to own a creative vision without adopting an autocratic style. One of the most important ways is to articulate a clear vision and direction, offer detailed and opinionated criticism during the concept development—and then, largely, let it go. I'll explain what I mean by "letting it go" through an example.

When I was the Vice President of Design at Blackboard, we launched the previously described product that helped college students find their way. I "led" the product; I articulated a very specific vision for why the product needed to exist, who would use it, how it would work, and how, generally, a student would experience it. I was able to articulate this vision in such detail because my team and I had been walking our way around the topic for years.

As the designers worked on it, we would critique it. We would discuss whether the design made sense in the context of the experience, and whether the design supported the value promise. I was very vocal in those conversations. I would probe and push on design decisions and constantly ask, "Why?" I would offer my opinion, typically framed as a statement— "That doesn't make sense, and here's why," or "That will be confusing, and here's why." I would stick my nose into whiteboard conversations, offer unsolicited suggestions, and generally, I was all over the designers.

Then we got to a stage where the concept became an articulated visual vision. We had something to look at and rally around. We had identified the roadmap: We knew what the product would do, how it would look, and how it would get built. We knew how someone would experience it. Our team now had a strong rationale for our design decisions.

At that point, my leadership shifted. Where I had been challenging the team, looking inwards, my role became to protect the team, looking outwards. During the detailed design work, product sprints, and execution, my focus was to remove obstacles and barriers so the team could do their work. I stayed somewhat involved with the vision and narrative because it's hard to stop advising when you see the product coming to life around you. But I didn't need to have the right answers; I didn't need to have any answers at all. I need to give the team the room to come up with their own answers.

This is *letting go*—allowing the team to take ownership of an idea.

TREAT PROJECT OWNERSHIP AS A STRATEGIC DECISION, KNOWING WHEN TO DRIVE AND WHEN TO STEP ASIDE.

BUILDING A CURRICULUM

As creativity grows in your organization, creative teams gain responsibility, and "non-creative" teams start to become curious and energized by what they see. There's a swarming of activity around creativity, as people can literally see the value of artifacts. Once they see diagrams and beautiful sketches and new ideas, they want some of that creative goodness. They want to be associated with that type of thinking, and they want to leverage those artifacts in their own groups.

This popularity broadens the team's responsibilities on a project. In addition to making the work, individual contributors are responsible for shepherding it through the organization. By gaining cultural capital, they've gained the "meta" responsibilities around creative work and have joined the ranks of creative direction. Their duties start to include stakeholder management, and timing, budgeting, and ownership of the result. They stop doing the work and start managing it.

This management is about teaching – and building a curriculum.

Teaching is a natural evolution. As creative teams start to flourish, members of the team become responsible for advocating for the work and giving the organization the context it needs to evaluate and consume it. Individual designers become leaders, not just practitioners.

The development of leadership in directing the creative process comes from experience. This creative leadership is based on knowing the right balance of hands-on and motivational guidance. It's similar to other forms of mentorship, but the differences lie in the production of an artifact. As a creative director, the expectation is that you know how to guide the team, but that you don't actually do the work yourself. When that line is crossed—when you start doing the work, or redoing your teams' work—your leadership degrades.

What specifically happens when that line is crossed is that junior employees grow into creative directors and, because they don't have rich experience to draw from, their creative direction is unsubstantiated. They compensate for their lack of experience with an anxious form of micromanaging, and their stress becomes contagious. This derails momentum for the team and erodes the trust the team has in their leadership.

Managing a creative staff requires a formal educational plan to teach method and process. I mean *actually* teaching, in a model that looks very similar to how a college might teach and college students might learn. With a formal curriculum developed, you can quickly grow junior talent, onboard large groups, and empower senior staff to gain leadership skills. You can help that newly minted creative director to gain the skills needed to succeed as a leader. This is similar to the teaching philosophy and methodology that Stephanie Wade pursued through government's Office of Personal Management: Her team didn't just *do creative work*, they also formally taught their process to other team members.

When I started teaching, I had no idea how to write a course plan, craft a syllabus, or create teaching materials. A former colleague (and a much more experienced professor) gave me some great teaching advice. He told me to treat education like a creative problem itself, and to leverage all of my design techniques to create a curriculum. For me, this meant sketching with a marker on a big sheet of paper, working through mind mapping, getting critique on my work, and iterating. I followed the methods I've described in this book.

First, I framed the problem by identifying opportunities, building a value promise, and structuring a view of course goals. Next, I iterated on the curriculum by having other educators review the work and critique it, cycling through a process of ideation. In a somewhat meta- fashion, I used the creative process to develop a curriculum to teach the creative process.

When I started sketching out my course plan, it was easy to get wrapped up in the breadth of content I needed to disseminate and to emphasize all the principles, theories, skills and methods I knew and wanted my teams to know. The sheer amount of content was intimidating, making it hard to actually get started.

So instead of focusing on the amount of content, my first problem frame was to think of the content as a means to an end, where my goal was immediate applicability. For each piece of content or method that I considered teaching, I asked, "why is this important to you? When will it be important to you? What are the circumstances in which you'll use this skill or consider this theory?" I emphasized relevance as a criterion to determine whether something should be in the curriculum.

When you craft a curriculum for your team, also visualize the end state—describe what you want your team to learn. In academia, end states are called "learning outcomes." These are the stuffy statements that say things like, "Achieved proficiency in…" or "Demonstrated a sound ability to…." But it's less important to write formal outcomes, and more important to consider what you want the team to learn on an achievable level. This forces you to shift from a broad view ("I want them to learn design") to a detailed one ("I want them to learn how to analyze complex problems") and then to an assessable one ("My creative teams will be able to analyze complex problems").

By starting at the end-state, you can envision how the team will change after experiencing your curricula: how they'll see the world differently, and how they'll act differently as a result of this new perspective. This is your opportunity statement and problem frame.

ESTABLISH A LEARNING CULTURE THAT FOCUSES ON A REAL CURRICULUM CENTERED AROUND APPLICABILITY.

FLEX TIME AND PASSION PROJECTS

A lot has been written about Google's flexible creative time—individual contributors are given 20% of their time to do whatever "…they think will most benefit Google," according to Founders Larry Page and Sergey Brin. "This empowers them to be more creative and innovative." (D'Onfro, 2015) Typically, engineers spend the time trying new projects, learning new technology, or participating in online and offline discussions about the role of engineering in the world. This flexible time is generally considered to be the source of innovations like Gmail and Google Earth.

Some people express skepticism that the concept really exists; Marissa Mayer, CEO of Yahoo and former employee of Google, famously said "I've got to tell you the dirty little secret of Google's 20% time. It's really 120% time." (Carlson, 2015) But even if the program isn't as formalized as it might appear, it's clear that the company's looser work-time regulations are an effort to accelerate innovation.

Not all companies can emulate the 20% time, and not all companies strive to build a culture like Google's. But creative burnout is real and ubiquitous, and companies struggle to find ways to manage the constant pressure to deliver.

Mike Kruzeniski is the Senior Director of Design at Twitter and a former creative lead at Microsoft and Nokia. He oversees a team of 35 designers, who work near the engineers responsible for shipping all aspects of Twitter. The teams work hard, he says, so to prevent creative burnout, he steers them towards three outlets for overcoming stress.

1. **Whole-strategy vision projects.** A vision project is an exploration of a beautiful, idealized future. Often describing five years out, the vision project is used to help teams extract themselves from the

minutia of product details. It is typically scenario-based, grounded in research, and without boundaries. Crazy ideas like invisibility cloaks are okay because the intent is not believability as much as persuasiveness. A vision project is great for motivating individual contributors, and the results often act as strong internal (and even external) marketing collateral.

But there's a downside, Kruzeniski says; vision projects can be "… all-encompassing to the point that everybody knows they're not achievable. It just doesn't make sense to build products like ours in that way, sort of like rethink[ing] everything all at once." Twitter can't stop what they are doing and suddenly unveil an entirely different product, so the team acknowledges these vision projects as inspirational but not practical.

Additionally, a blue-sky vision project runs the risk of alienating people knee-deep in shipping products. "One team is saying, 'These guys don't get it. They don't get what it means to actually go build a product,'" Kruzeniski says. "And the other team is going 'These guys don't get it. They're not thinking about the future.'"

2. **What-if projects.** A second form of exploratory project asks and answers, "what if?" about a specific product feature or capability. The creative team tries to provoke a lot of new iterations by considering what would happen if a business, technology, or design constraint were removed. These questions aren't aimed at actual implementation work—the intent is to create a series of open-ended vignettes.

These projects can focus on the UI (user interface) or more conceptually on the actual product capabilities. Kruzeniski offered two examples of "what-if" provocations:

What if Twitter had no tabs, and were just a timeline view? Twitter's web client displays "Home," "Moments," "Notifications," "Messages," and "Search" as destinations within the product. What if it didn't—how would the product change with that simpler set of capabilities?

What if Twitter were only for self-expression? People use Twitter for a variety of activities, including reading news, participating in conversations, and expressing themselves. What if the product were optimized for self-expression—how would it change?

3. **Making a physical thing.** Kruzeniski says that he often has his teams take breaks from their digital product work to make a physical item, like a book. He said a physical item is fast to make, inclusive, and harnesses a carefree form of creativity that isn't always present in real product work. "There's less on the line. There's a lot of stress in building real products, you have a lot on the line as far as the business and how users are going to adopt it or not adopt it. And all of that stuff is really important, but it can be stressful. Something as simple as a book feels like more raw creative."

    This artifact—a book, a poster, or a research report—can end up as a beautiful representation of the team's culture. It celebrates the people doing the work, the environment in which the work is made, and the process of the work as much as the output. "Go work on a book that tells the story of where the studio is at, at this moment in time. That stuff is like a little time capsule of who we were, how we think, and what we believed in, in this moment in time." (Kruzeniski, 2016)

    Joe Gebbia at Airbnb made a similar artifact about the team and about their shared vision. "At the beginning of the year, we did an exercise where I asked each member of the product team (engineers, designers, producers) to email me their favorite customer testimonial from…a guest or host on Airbnb that they connected with the most… We took all of those stories and bound them in a book and sent it back to the entire team. The book gave a lens into the types of things we could be creating together."

These types of "free time" projects seem incidental and might appear to be a waste of time. But they serve three main purposes.

First, they offer contributors a way to temper feelings of resentment towards their project, as an alternative to quitting. Often, time heals wounds, and after completing a passion project like the ones described above, an employee can come back to work recharged.

Next, these types of projects signal a culture that celebrates creative exploration. They highlight that not all creative activities need to be productive and show the team that management recognizes and appreciates creativity as an end in itself. Even books and posters serve a tangible purpose, as they can be held up to the world as signals of the company's commitment to creativity.

Finally, the output of these projects *is* materially valuable. Vision work, both at a tactical level and at a broad blue-sky level, establishes and refines the trajectory of a team, and acts as a point of alignment for product road-mapping.

TO HELP YOUR TEAM REMAIN INSPIRED, DEDICATE TIME TO ALTERNATIVE PROJECTS, AND TREAT THEM AS IMPORTANT AS "MAIN" PROJECTS.

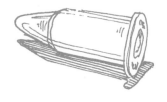

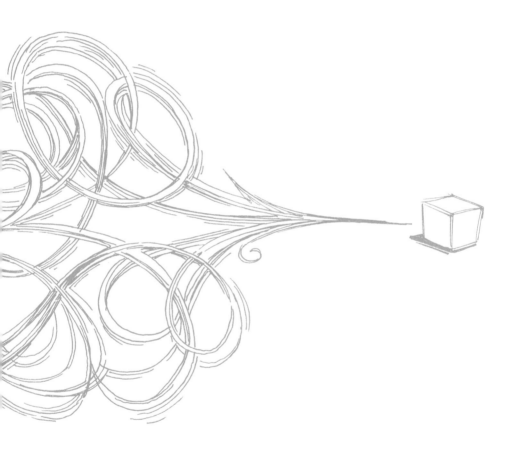

SUMMARY

Throughout this book, we have explored ideas related to constraints, iteration, critique, trust, and confidence. These topics all focus on the idea of creative clarity. Creativity is such a strong force that, left unmanaged, it will rip through your business and cause chaos and strife. But by taming ambiguity through the creative methods described, you can start to see a clear path towards creative success.

Finding creative clarity means driving an iterative process of exploration and lateral thinking. A creative problem is ambiguous and without edges, and the creative process helps provide structure around that ambiguity. That exploration happens through narrative and storytelling, through diagramming and prototyping, and through problem framing. One of the most important parts of that framing is articulating a vision, so that the team drives towards a north star.

Creative clarity requires critique and criticism. Your team needs to hear when their creations don't work, and they need to hear that feedback in a structured environment. That environment is characterized by a unique form of trust, in which it's ok to show vulnerability while taking ownership of creative failures. You've seen how to build trust, encourage ownership, teach through apprenticeship, and help your team find inspiration.

You've also learned that you can't leave creative clarity to chance. You must strategically consider a creative environment; you must foster and respect it. Creativity has become a fundamental part of business, so treat it like the fundamental competency that it is.

In a creative environment, chaos is the backdrop for hidden wonderment and success. You now have the skills, language, methods, and process to gain clarity in the face of that chaos, so you can build great products, great teams, and a high-performing creative organization.

ACKNOWLEDGEMENTS

I would like to thank the following people, who played an instrumental role in bringing this book to life:

- Paul Burke, who was responsible for the great visual aesthetic of the book itself

- Austin Rucker, who developed the awesome illustrations you've seen throughout the text

- Ronnie Lipton, for helping me shape my words and thoughts

- Ben Fullerton, Brian Romanko, Chris Risdon, Evan Torchin, Ivo Stivoric, Judy Siegel, Kevin McDonald, Mark Rolston, Mike Albers, Mike Kruzeniski, Rachel Hinman, and Stephanie Wade, for sharing their experiences and helping me frame my understanding of creativity

- My mom, for a sanity check

- Matt Franks, Chad Fisher, and Patrick Marsh, for supporting my work

And, most importantly,

- Jess, my wife - for patience and endless support.

WORKS CITED

Bariso, J. (n.d.). "Steve Jobs Brainstorms With the NeXT Team." Retrieved from *Inc.*: http://www.inc.com/justin-bariso/8-essential-lessons-from-this-meeting-led-by-a-young-steve-jobs.html

Bass, L., Kasabch, C., Martin, R., Siewiorek, D., Smailagic, A., & Stivoric, J. (1997). "The Design of a Wearable Computer." *CHI.*

Berkun, S. (2004, 06 01). "How To Survive Creative Burnout." Retrieved from Scott Berkun: http://scottberkun.com/essays/33-how-to-survive-creative-burnout/

Beryl, L. (2014, 07 02). "What Being a VC Taught Me About Entrepreneurship." Retrieved from NBC News: http://www.nbcnews.com/id/55553201/ns/business-small_business/t/what-being-vc-taught-me-about-entrepreneurship/#.WIzUyFMrKMo

Calnan, C. (2013, 11 06). "How IBM is Keeping It Weird for Tech Design in Austin; Is This a Startup or Big Blue?" Retrieved from *Austin Business Journal:* http://www.bizjournals.com/austin/blog/techflash/2013/11/ibm-is-keeping-it-weird-for-tech-design.html

Carlson, N. (2015, Jan 13). "The 'Dirty Little Secret' About Google's 20% Time, According To Marissa Mayer." Retrieved from *Business Insider:* http://www.businessinsider.com/mayer-google-20-time-does-not-exist-2015-1

Chung, M. (2013, 11 14). "Under Armour Buying MapMyFitness in $150 Million Deal." Retrieved from Bloomberg: http://www.bloomberg.com/news/articles/2013-11-14/under-armour-to-buy-fitness-technology-company-for-150-million

Crissey, M. (2005, 05 28). "Improved Gadgets Help Exercisers See the Burn." Retrieved from *USA Today:* http://usatoday30.usatoday.com/tech/products/gear/2005-05-28-fitness-gadgets_x.htm

Dolan, B. (2011, 06 30). "Why BodyMedia Will Be the First of Many Acquisitions." Retrieved from *Mobi Health News:* http://mobihealthnews.com/11574/why-bodymedia-will-be-the-first-of-many-acquisitions

D'Onfro, J. (2015, 04 17). "The truth about Google's famous '20% time' policy." Retrieved from *Business Insider:* http://www.businessinsider.com/google-20-percent-time-policy-2015-4

Eames, C. (2016, 08 04). "Design Q&A Text." Retrieved from Eames Official Site: http://www.eamesoffice.com/the-work/design-q-a-text/

Earnest. (2017, Jan 29). Retrieved from Earnest: https://www.earnest.com/

Foster, T. (2016, 02). "Kevin Plank Is Betting Almost $1 Billion That Under Armour Can Beat Nike." Retrieved from *Inc.*: http://www.inc.com/ magazine/201602/tom-foster/kevin-plank-under-armour-spending- 1-billion-to-beat-nike.html

Fullerton, B. (2016, July 18). Interview. (J. Kolko, Interviewer)

Gebbia, J. (2013, July 8). Interview. (J. Kolko, Interviewer)

Gedenryd, H. (1998). How Designers Work. (unpublished).

Gemperle, F., Kasabach, C., Stivoric, J., Bauer, M., & Martin, R. (1998). "Design for Wearability."

Germano, S. (2015, 02 04). "Under Armour Acquires MyFitnessPal for $475 Million." Retrieved from *The Wall Street Journal*: http://www.wsj.com/articles/ under-armour-to-acquire-myfitnesspal-for-475-million-1423086478

Gianatasio, D. (2015, January 6). "How a 2009 Interview With Ira Glass Still Inspires Struggling Young Creatives Today." Retrieved from *Adweek*: http://www.adweek.com/creativity/how-2009-interview- ira-glass-still-inspires-struggling-young-creatives-today-162177/

Jones, B. (2013, 10 31). "Leadership Lessons From Walt Disney: Letting Go." Retrieved from The Disney Institute: https://disneyinstitute.com/blog/2013/10/ leadership-lessons-from-walt-disney-letting-go/211/

Kalil, T. (2015, September 4). "Using Human-Centered Design to Make Government Work Better and Cost Less." Retrieved from the White House: https://www.whitehouse.gov/blog/2015/09/04/using-human-centered-design-make-government-work-better-and-cost-less

Khan, B. (2012, December 2). "Rapid Prototyping, the Google X Way." Retrieved from Mind The Product: http://www.mindtheproduct.com/2012/12/rapid-prototyping-the-google-x-way/

Kolko, J. (2016, 07 13). "Announcing Bb Planner: A Path to Student Success." Retrieved from Blackboard Blog: http://blog.blackboard.com/announcing-bb-planner-a-product-for-student-success/

Kovatech, K. (1994, 04 27). "Sandbox Technologies Spins Off from CMU." Retrieved from *Pittsburgh Business Times:* http://www.bizjournals.com/pittsburgh/stories/1998/04/27/focus2.html

Kruzeniski, M. (2016, 07 29). Interview. (J. Kolko, Interviewer)

Markoff, J. (1996, March 11). "Nothing Up Their Sleeves? Masters of the High Tech Demo Spin Their Magic." Retrieved from *The New York Times:* http://www.nytimes.com/1996/03/11/business/nothing-up-their-sleeves-masters-of-the-high-tech-demo-spin-their-magic.html

McConnell, S. (2011, January 9). "Origins of 10X—How Valid is the Underlying Research?" Retrieved from Construx: http://www.construx.com/10x_Software_Development/Origins_of_10X_%E2%80%93_How_Valid_is_the_Underlying_Research_/

Murphy, V. (2005, 06 06). "Future Teller." Retrieved from *Forbes:* http://www.forbes.com/free_forbes/2005/0606/071.html

Musk, E. (2016, 07 20). "Master Plan, Part Deux." Retrieved from Tesla: https://www.tesla.com/blog/master-plan-part-deux

Pacifico, N. (2016, July 12). "Federal Improper Payments Are Significant, Costing Taxpayers Billions." Retrieved from Project on Government Oversight: http://www.pogo.org/our-work/reports/2016/introduction-to-improper-payments.html?referrer=https://www.google.com/

Paul Pugh. (2015, 04 02). Retrieved from The Design Lens: https://thedesignlens.com/tag/paul-pugh/

Pierce, D. (2016, 01 05). "How Under Armour Plans to Turn Your Clothes Into Gadgets." Retrieved from *Wired:* http://www.wired.com/2016/01/under-armour-healthbox/

Rolston, M. (2016, 07 21). Interview. (J. Kolko, Interviewer)

Ryan, P. (2015, 04 24). "Capital One: Think More Like a Tech Company, Less Like a Bank." Retrieved from *Bank Innovation:* http://bankinnovation.net/2015/04/capital-one-think-more-like-a-tech-company-less-like-a-bank/

Shah, A. (2014, January 15). "Blackboard Buys Austin Edtech Startup MyEdu for Student Profiles." Retrieved from *xconomy:* http://www.xconomy.com/texas/2014/01/15/blackboard-buys-austin-edtech-startup-myedu-for-student-profiles/#

Shieber, J. (2015, November 17). "Lending Company Earnest Raises $275 Million As FinTech Remains In The Spotlight." Retrieved from *TechCrunch*: https://techcrunch.com/2015/11/17/lending-company-earnest-raises-275-million-as-fintech-remains-in-the-spotlight/

Steele, B. (2015, 02 04). "Under Armour Spent Half a Billion Dollars on Two Fitness Apps." Retrieved from Engadget: https://www.engadget.com/2015/02/04/under-armour-acquires-endomondo-myfitnesspal/

Torchin, E. (2016, 07 09). Interview. (J. Kolko, Interviewer)

Trites, D. (n.d.). "How Under Armour's Digital Transformation Will Improve Your Health." Retrieved from SAP: https://news.sap.com/how-under-armours-digital-transformation-will-improve-your-health/

Under Armour. (n.d.). "Under Armour Connected Fitness." Retrieved from Under Armour Connected Fitness: https://www.underarmour.com/en-us/ua-record

USDA. (2013, September). "National School Lunch Program—Fact Sheet." Retrieved from USDA Food and Nutrition Service: https://www.fns.usda.gov/sites/default/files/NSLPFactSheet.pdf

USDA. (2015). "Free and Reduced Price School Meals Application." Retrieved from USDA Food and Nutrition Service: https://www.fns.usda.gov/sites/default/files/english.pdf

Velazco, C. (2013, 04 30). "Jawbone Acquires BodyMedia For Over $100 Million To Give It An Edge In Wearable Health Tracking." Retrieved from TechCrunch: https://techcrunch.com/2013/04/30/ jawbone-will-acquire-bodymedia-for-over-100-million-to-give-it-an-edge-in-wearable-health-tracking/

Verry, P. (2016, 05 04). "Kevin Plank Opens Up About Data, Innovation & Future Plans At Under Armour." Retrieved from *Footwear News*: http://footwearnews.com/2016/influencers/power-players/ kevin-plank-under-armour-ceo-technology-data-innovation-216505/

Wade, S. (2017, Jan 02). Interview. (J. Kolko, Interviewer)

Wilson, M. (2014, 03 27). "IBM Invests $100 Million To Expand Design Business." Retrieved from *Fast Company*: http://www.fastcodesign. com/3028271/ibm-invests-100-million-to-expand-design-business

Wysocki, B. (2001, 04 17). "BodyMedia Tries to Sell Health Care With High-Tech Style to Insurers." Retrieved from *The Wall Street Journal*: https://www.wsj.com/articles/SB987459566451890634

X, G. (2016, 20 12). "About X." Retrieved from Google X: https://x. company/about

Zhuo, J. (2014, January 21). "Why Designers Leave." Retrieved from Medium: https://medium.com/the-year-of-the-looking-glass/ why-designers-leave-d0aa3b8af9b7#.7amuvelm1